The Expert Editor

Tips, Advice, Insights, and Solutions

W0007993

Editorial Experts, Inc.

The Expert Editor

Tips, Advice, Insights, and Solutions

Ann R. Molpus
Editor

EDITORIAL EXPERTS, INC.

Other books published by Editorial Experts, Inc.:

Substance & Style: Instruction and Practice in Copyediting, by Mary Stoughton

Mark My Words: Instruction and Practice in Proofreading, by Peggy Smith

Simplified Proofreading, by Peggy Smith

Stet! Tricks of the Trade for Writers and Editors, edited by Bruce O. Boston

Language On A Leash, by Bruce O. Boston

Directory of Editorial Resources

For information, write

Editorial Experts, Inc.
66 Canal Center Plaza, Suite 200
Alexandria, VA 22314-1538
Attn: Publications Division
703-683-0683

Table of Contents

Preface

The Expert Editor incorporates some of the most valuable insights, hints, and suggestions that the staff of Editorial Experts, Inc., has gleaned on the job and from other publications professionals during the past 18 years.

Founded in 1972, Editorial Experts, Inc. (EEI), is the oldest and largest editorial consulting firm on the East Coast. Over the years, we have watched the publications business change dramatically through the introduction of new technologies. While embracing the new, we also realize that the ultimate success of a publication remains rooted in the timeless principles of good writing, thoughtful editing, and a definable purpose for the publication. The articles in this book reflect those principles. The first section, "Starting Out," discusses issues every new editor should ponder and every experienced editor should review periodically. The second, "Policies, Procedures, and People," covers the practical issues with which every editor grapples daily. The third, "Levels and Types of Editing," offers guidelines for editing under varying circumstances.

Since 1978, we have reported on the changing publications scene and offered advice to editing professionals through our award-winning monthly newsletter, *The Editorial Eye*. We have compiled some of the *Eye* articles that deal with the fundamentals of the editing process in *The Expert Editor*. By collecting these classic articles here, we hope to give editors a framework for their professional skills that will remain constant regardless of technology.

Ann R. Molpus
Editor
November 1990

Starting Out

by Priscilla S. Taylor

Do You Have What It Takes to Be a Great Editor?

A twelve-point litmus test for people who work with words

A. Scott Berg, in his biography of *Max Perkins: Editor of Genius*, has described a rare occasion when this consummate American book editor was persuaded to "give a few words on the subject" of editors and editing before some students taking a university extension course on book publishing in 1946.

Although Perkins was virtually unknown outside the publishing world, he was noted inside that world for his astute literary judgment and his ability to inspire authors to produce their best. He had discovered and encouraged talents such as F. Scott Fitzgerald, Ernest Hemingway, and Thomas Wolfe. His credo was "The book belongs to the author," and he opened his remarks to the students that night by saying, "The first thing you must remember [is] an editor does not add to a book. At best, he serves as a handmaiden to an author. Don't ever get to feeling important about yourself, because an editor at most releases energy. He creates nothing." Although Perkins was being a bit disingenuous on this occasion, the advice remains valid.

What personal qualities characterize a good editor? Berg says that the two qualities that distinguish the professional editor are "the vision to see beyond the faults of a good book, no matter how dismaying; and the tenacity to keep working, through all discouragements, toward the book's potential." Master stylist E.B. White once mentioned "taste, judgment, and education" as essential in handling the English language. Here are a few other desirable characteristics for editors:

▲ *A love of words and a passion for seeing them used precisely.* Robert MacNeil, cohost of public television's "Mac-Neil/Lehrer Newshour" and coauthor of the TV series and book *The Story of English*, has described in a memoir called *Wordstruck* how his love of language began in childhood, as his mother read to him with drama and enthusiasm a poem by Robert Louis Stevenson. "The way the words were read, and where, and when," he says, began to shape his deep feeling for language.

▲ *An interest in detail.* If an author says a list will contain seven items, it's important to make sure that there are seven, that they are presented in parallel style, and that the author has discussed them in the order in which they were listed. Similarly, the editor must be willing to check each table against the text that describes it, making sure they agree.

I include under this "interest in detail" an ability to spell, or a willingness to look words up and check them out. Good spelling alone won't make anyone a good editor, but if there's one thing authors rely on editors to save them from, it's misspelling.

▲ *A healthy skepticism.* "Interestingly....," says the author. "Let the reader judge," says the editor.

▲ *A good memory.* Editors must be attuned to repetition so they can trim it.

▲ *A love of reading and an eagerness to learn new things and master new subjects.*

▲ *A certain amount of tact to work well with all kinds of authors,* most of whom will view a new editor's work with suspicion. Working in black pencil rather than red pen, for example, subtly indicates that whatever is being suggested is just that—a suggestion. I like to give brief marginal explanations of any editorial changes for which the rationale may not be self-evident. A page-by-page covering memo may be necessary for heavily edited material.

▲ *Self-confidence.* Editors have to develop confidence in themselves so that they can project confidence to others. Editors develop this confidence by knowing their stuff thoroughly and having a reason for everything they do. Then they can demonstrate that they are improving the author's handiwork.

▲ *A good measure of flexibility to roll with the punches—to know when to quit.* Excellence is a realistic goal; perfection is not. Editors can go quietly mad seeking perfection.

▲ *A highly developed sense of proportion.* All things are not equally important. Accuracy and removal of ambiguity are worth fighting for; a particular style of capitalization or punctuation usually is not.

Similarly, although it's important to edit out language that will offend readers, it's also important to avoid jumping on every linguistic bandwagon. An association handbook I worked on specified that the meeting place should be "accessible to the physically challenged," meaning disabled. It seemed to me that "accessible to everybody" got the point across better.

▲ *A sense of humor.* Try to protect the author from appearing ridiculous in print. For example, a government report I edited attributed the food poisoning of the Vikings football team on an airline to "sandwiches that had been subjected to temperature abuse." This seemed a convoluted way of saying the food had not been properly refrigerated.

▲ *Clarity of thought and an interest in working with other people's thoughts.* I subscribe to Max Perkins's avowed view that the editor's task is basically derivative rather than creative, although some editorial solutions to writing problems may be quite creative. Indeed, for years scholars have been arguing over whether Perkins was too creative in his editing of Thomas Wolfe for Scribner's, and whether Wolfe's last editor, Edward Aswell, at Harper's, took too many liberties in organizing Wolfe's vast creative outpouring into the works published after his death. A book called *Thomas Wolfe and His Editors*, by Purdue University professor Leslie Field, absolves both editors, proclaiming that they served Wolfe well.

This is how Field describes the kind of changes Aswell made in the posthumous works:

> *Stylistic changes to achieve coherence and consistency and to eliminate irrelevancies, changes to alter characters' names [Wolfe kept changing his protagonist's name!], and changes to tone down excessive obscenity and vituperation.... Where Wolfe became repetitive, several lines may [have been] cut and the portions leading into and away from the bloated pieces interwoven.... Epithets for Jews and other minorities were generally excised.*

It's hard to quibble with changes like those.

▲ *A self-effacing personality.* Editors generally have to be content with a cursory acknowledgment in the introduction as their only public reward. It's the author who'll get the book prize.

©1989 Priscilla S. Taylor. This article is excerpted from remarks by the author, who gave the Phi Beta Kappa address on editing and a liberal arts education at Agnes Scott College in April 1989.

What Editors and Writers Should Know

Ask these questions before you pick up a pencil

I f you want a realistic estimate of the time and cost involved in a writing or an editing job, you need certain basic information about the project. Here are some questions to help you clarify any assignment.

What Editors Need to Know

In addition to such basics as the purpose and audience of the final product, editors need to know the following:

1. How many pages are in the existing manuscript? Are they single spaced or double spaced? (or, heaven forbid, handwritten?) Is the manuscript expected to be significantly shorter in its final form?

2. Does the manuscript contain tables, footnotes, equations, bibliography, charts, graphs, or other nontext material? If so, roughly how much such material is there?

3. Can the editor arrange to look at the manuscript to see what work will be needed? Some manuscripts are fairly well written and need only a relatively light editing for grammar, spelling, and consistency; others need many changes—almost a total rewrite—to be readable. Most editors will want to see for themselves how much and what kind of work will be required.

4. Exactly what tasks will be required? Will the editor be responsible for marking typefaces and sizes for the typesetter? Will the editor be expected to check math in tables? To verify all bibliographic entries at the library?

5. Has a graphics designer already been chosen to design the document and prepare any charts, cover art, and illustrations? Will the editor be expected to find someone to perform those tasks?

6. If photos or other illustrations will be used, who will provide and select them?

7. Does the client have a preference for a particular style on such matters as capitalization, punctuation, and hyphenation (e.g., Vice-Chairman or vice chairman)?

8. Will the original author review the editor's changes? If so, will the editor need to meet with the author?

9. Who will review the editor's work?

10. Will there be more than one cycle of review and revision?

11. Will the project director or the author be available to answer questions as the editing progresses?

12. Is there a firm outline that the manuscript should follow, or can the editor move sections around if a transfer seems to help the flow?

13. What are the chances that the author will want to make changes midway in the editing process—for example, dropping or adding sections?

14. In what condition should the manuscript be returned? Marked up with changes on the original, or keyed?

15. What is the condition of any illustrations that will accompany the manuscript? Finished art, rough sketches, suggestions?

What Writers Need to Know

1. What will the final product be? A book, a speech, a brochure, a handbook, a script?

2. Who is the primary audience? The general public, interested organizations, experts in the field?

3. What purpose will the document serve? What will the audience use it for? Why is it needed?

4. Roughly how long should the finished product be?

5. Has anyone already done any work on the project? If so, what shape are things in? Is there already a rough draft, or is there only a collection of raw material to work with? If someone's previous draft was rejected, what was wrong with it?

6. Is there an outline that shows exactly what topics will be covered, or is that something the writer will be expected to produce?

7. If the writer must do interviews or gather raw material and background information, who must be interviewed and where is the material? Who can answer the contractor's questions about needed information?

8. If the writer must attend conferences or meetings, how much time is likely to be required? Do the other people involved in the meetings have particular times they will or will not be available?

9. If tape recordings are to be provided as part of the background material, will they be transcribed or not?

10. Who will review the writer's drafts? One person, a committee, outside readers?

11. How many cycles of review and revision are expected?

12. Is there a firm deadline for the final product?

—Test Yourself—

-mancy Words

See if you can match these terms for "scrying" or divining the future (from *descry*, to catch sight of) with their "speculum" or medium.

1. chiromancy		a.	mirror
2. necromancy		b.	spring water
3. catoptromancy		c.	crystals
4. crystallomancy		d.	fingernails
5. pegomancy		e.	palms
6. lithomancy		f.	stones
7. onychomancy		g.	departed spirits
8. lecanomancy		h.	wrinkles in the belly
9. rhabdomancy		i.	full water basin
10. gastromancy		j.	divining rod

Answers on p. 96.

by Ann R. Molpus

Hints from the
Washingtonian

Editor Jack Limpert shares lessons he learned the hard way

" Even the best editors get flak—it comes with the territory," says Jack Limpert, editor of *Washingtonian* magazine. Limpert says he let the criticism bother him for many years until he realized that an editor has to learn from mistakes and move on.

Limpert offers other insights gained during 20 years as editor of *Washingtonian*. The most important thing to remember is that "in all decisions, an editor's primary goal should be to serve the readers and enhance the publication. Every editorial decision should be made with regard to improving the product put before the readers."

Because readers are busy people who already have too much to read, Limpert says they "graze" through publications. If anything about an article is confusing, they move on. The editor must make sure each article is appealing and direct enough to make some segment of the audience stop and read. Strong headlines, dramatic photos, eye-catching call-outs, and informative photo captions pull readers into articles.

To develop interesting editorial material, an editor must build a connection with the readers by understanding their interests and needs, and learning to speak their language. The editor should appeal to the readers' self-interest by presenting practical, usable information that helps them stay not only on top of trends but one step ahead. Photos, in-depth articles, or profiles can take readers where they can't go themselves. "Editors and writers are interested in turmoil and trouble; readers aren't," Limpert says. Editors must present stories in an honest but positive manner. Whether the topic is finding affordable health care or an honest auto mechanic, problems should be acknowledged and solutions suggested.

Limpert urges editors not to be slaves to detail. He believes that it is more important to spend time talking with your staff and the publication's audience than rifling through an "in" box. He admits that he is still a very involved manager; he reviews all story assignments and design concepts and reads galleys for each issue. But he also hires bright people with strengths he lacks and gives them freedom to make their own decisions.

Further, he encourages *Washingtonian* editors to write periodically so that they can appreciate their freelancers. "Editors can easily become disgruntled with freelancers unless they understand what the writer goes through," he says. Freelancers' insights are valuable because they often serve as an editor's eyes and ears in the outside world. Without them, Limpert says, "you end up talking to yourself."

When in doubt about an article, a cover illustration, or a management issue, Limpert advises editors to say "no" or "no, but I'll think about it." "You can always change your position from 'no' to 'yes' but not vice versa," he explains. Nor do editors always need logical reasons for saying "no"; instincts are usually correct.

Editors must create a sense of teamwork and family among staff members and between departments. Limpert keeps an open door, circulates frequently through the office, acknowledges good work, and remembers birthdays and job anniversaries. He also organizes regular working lunches for specific groups within the staff. To maintain good communication with the advertising department, he meets informally with the sales staff each month before they start selling. He provides editorial information around which the salespeople can build advertising for the next issue.

by Mara T. Adams

How Do You "Be" an Editor?

*The essence of a good editor's character
is part temperament, part training*

With this question, a participant in one of Editorial Experts' seminars condemned me to hours of philosophical contemplation. What did she mean? What could she have meant: How does one set out to become an editor? How does one act as an editor? What is an editor? How does an editor think? Metaphysics aside, the question of how one "be's" an editor is intriguing because, as all editors know, the roads that lead to the practice of our craft are as various as its tasks and skills. I have chosen to interpret *be* in its sense of essence.

Temperament

Editors are seekers of that perfect harmony that Renaissance philosophers called "the music of the spheres." They are critics in the purest sense, those who aspire to judge and discern the words that jar and the sentences that don't make sense. But if you lack the inborn quirks of character that combine diffidence with arrogance, poetry with logic, and flexibility with compulsion, the best you can hope to be is a grammarian. Given grammatical knowledge of the language, the editor must also possess two other qualities: an intuitive understanding of how words work together to achieve their best expression and an implacable conviction that the piece of writing does not exist that cannot be improved.

The occupational hazard of most editors is that they may never stop working—reading for pleasure is to them both the ultimate redundancy *and* the ultimate contradiction in terms. Yet common sense and authors' sensibilities demand that the editorial

11

workhorse be hobbled. The editor therefore needs the sense of proportion and of balance that translates into knowing when to stop. Hence the lesson every editor must learn: Not every piece of writing needs or deserves the same level of editorial attention.

Training

Editorial training begins with an emotional attachment to the written word. By that I mean, the natural editor will read anything—poetry, history, trash novels, maps, dictionaries, comic strips, and the backs of cereal boxes—for the sheer joy of reading. Word games (remember "Botticelli"?) and crossword puzzles add to the cache of minutiae editors love to squirrel away. Acquiring the elements of style, consistency, accuracy, and clarity is simply a more elaborate word game, whose rules are set forth in dozens of reference works and whose object is to achieve encyclopedic knowledge of the lore of putting words on paper properly. (A college roommate once paid me the compliment of saying I possessed the largest store of useless information she had ever encountered.)

There is no one perfect way to train an editor, any more than there is one perfect way to train roses or children or puppies. Some cut their teeth directly on a manuscript, others on charts and tables, still others on verifying citations. For many, it's a matter of luck—landing in the right place at the right time; getting to know an old-fashioned editor who is willing to teach; reading, reading, and reading some more; or simply being thrown into the soup and finding the way out by instinct.

Whatever the method, the education of an editor is never complete. Every new manuscript, every new author, every new book has something to teach, and the natural editor is panting to learn it. In his wonderful little book, *The Elements of Editing*, Arthur Plotnik explains the compulsion that drives the editor:

> *The art of editing has more to do with felicity—with making just the right improvement to create light, joy, song, aptness, grace, beauty, or excitement where it wasn't quite happening.*

Not even the prestigious Radcliffe Publishing Procedures course can teach you that.

by Bruce O. Boston

The Editor as Seed Crystal

If it weren't for writers, most editors would be slinging hash

O n the theory that editors are just as narcissistic as the general population, and that we enjoy talking about ourselves just as much as failed actors and newly engaged couples, this article holds up the mirror to our sacred profession. The question is, what do we actually do?

First, since the glass doesn't lie, let's admit the truth. Despite the justifiable pride we may take in our craft, the living of an editor, like that of a book reviewer, is basically derivative. If it weren't for writers, most of us would be slinging hash instead of ink. Nonetheless, our profession does have standing of its own. There is some comfort, for example, in learning that—in English, at least—the verb *edit* did not come first, followed by the noun *editor*, as one might think. The *Oxford English Dictionary (OED)* reveals that *edit* is a back-formation from *editor*. (The *OED*'s first usage citation for *edit* is dated 1793; the first citation for *editor* is dated 1648.) This chronology does not necessarily mean that who we are takes precedence over what we do. It only revalidates the eternal truth that the ways of language are mysterious and there is no accounting for how some things get started.

A New Profession

Which brings us to point number two: Compared to a number of other professions, editing hasn't really been around all that long. It is only since the early eighteenth century that editors have been understood as persons who prepare the literary work of others for publication by a process of selection and revision. For about 150 years before that, *editor* was synonymous with *publisher*. Apparently, the assumption was that authors didn't need any help

13

with their writing, only with the less savory task of getting it before the public. Thus, from the beginning, we editors have been in the mercantile mire. Knowledge of one's origins is a great antidote for professional hubris.

But like any useful new idea, the notion of an editor has caught on and gone from strength to strength. Like engineering, medicine, law, and theology, editing has proliferated specializations, continually rejustifying its precarious existence on the fringes of literature. There are acquisitions editors, line editors, copyeditors, photo editors, technical editors, abstract editors, style editors, story editors, general editors, and to supervise them all, editors-in-chief. Thus, editors have become like doctors; you don't know without asking what any of them really does.

Dinner with the Queen

What most editors mostly do (we're talking about the ones who do *not* get to take authors to lunch at Elaine's or the Four Seasons) is to read manuscripts with pencil in hand, correcting the errors of organization and presentation that may confuse a reader, offend the canons of standard English usage and grammar, or aggravate the ulcer of a printer.

If that sounds like a piece of cake, you either do not understand editing at all or have not been doing it very long. The main problem with our profession, as William Bridgewater, former editor-in-chief of Columbia University Press, has pointed out, is that it is a task without thoroughly set limits. In other words, in editing, as in dressing to go to dinner with the Queen, it's hard to know when you're "ready." And, truth to tell, more than anything else, what defines "ready" is that your manuscript, like your person at the palace, has a time beyond which, if it doesn't show up, embarrasses everyone connected with the enterprise. You most of all.

Message and Medium

My own view of editing is a little more exciting than that, however. For me, editing is an immersion in the endlessly fascinating chemistry of the English language. I have yet to meet the editor who is really as self-absorbed as my tongue-in-cheek introduction to this column makes out. In truth, there is nothing editors care about so much as the endless possibilities for combination and recombination in language, and finding the right set of combinations for a particular manuscript. This passion is usually put in terms of the editor's responsibility to the author; what we really *must* care about is creating that arrangement of the author's words that best expresses the author's intention. What we seek is a kind of harmony, a crystallization in which message and medium merge.

When we do our jobs right, editors are like seed crystals. In chemistry, crystals are regular forms which seem to arise spontaneously and then replicate themselves in a stable manner. What sets this process off is a "seed crystal," which, when inserted into an assortment of molecules, brings those molecules together in a unique formation. Once the seed crystal is inserted, the molecules buzz around until, almost miraculously, they find the perfect arrangement to express exactly what they are. The result is maximum order and stability, in which all the molecules are organized in a way that leads to their continued existence. That's a job description for an editor if I ever heard one.

The Unattainable Triad

Time, quality, budget—you can only have two out of three

A good way to educate people who make demands on you as an editor but who understand little of the publication process is to explain the principle of "The Unattainable Triad." The three elements of this publications triad are time, money, and quality.

A good editorial manager can deliver two of the three elements; delivering all three is out of the question because the elements at the triangle's points pull in different directions.

For example, a combination of low funding and short time requires some compromises on quality. As one editor says, "You can have it right or you can have it right now, but you can't have both."

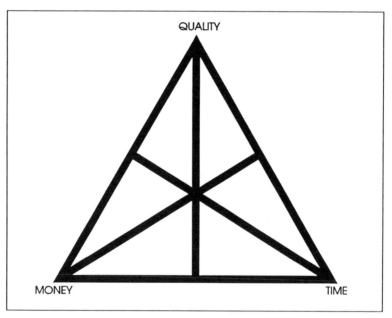

The Unattainable Triad

by Mary J. Scroggins

Are There Such Things as Editorial Absolutes?

If you want definitive answers to editing questions, you might be disappointed

I was once a humble editorial trainee. Like most new editors, I had no formal training in writing or grammar and only a vague idea of what an editor was. I ventured into this new profession anticipating that I would be privy to all the editorial secrets and dictates contained in the 2,003 resource books (a conservative exaggeration) dumped on my desk by the training manager. These books surely had the definitive answers to all my questions on writing, editing, and the English language. I was entering the land of "absolutes."

I had the good fortune to train in a company with a style guide that could hold its own against the *U.S. Government Printing Office (GPO) Style Manual* or *The Chicago Manual of Style*. Little could be left to choice or free will, I thought in my naiveté. I assumed that everything would fit neatly into a mold, pattern, style, or system. Surely these books contained rules to fit every need of every manuscript I would ever encounter.

Much to my dismay, aside from strict rules of grammar and widely accepted points of style, the number of "absolutes" decreased as my editing skills increased. Reality set in; I had to think, make choices, and do more than flip to page 204 and follow example 4.3. The resource books and house style guide served as the framework for my task of clarifying the language.

Recently—and not for the first time—a participant in an editing workshop that I conducted for Editorial Experts, Inc., asked for *the*

17

answer after almost every exercise. My answer—"That's good" (meaning, "You have improved the sentence and made it easier for the reader to understand. There are other ways to approach it, and we'll explore a few.")—would not do. I almost always followed my answer with a question: "How did other people in the class handle this sentence?" Again and again, this persistent woman, new to editing and still in search of absolutes, said, "Those are the choices; what's *the answer?*" The first few times she asked this, I responded with a lecture on the wonder, beauty, choices, and variations of the language. Note the emphasis on "choices" and "variations."

Those lectures can be summed up briefly: "There are no absolutes."

The lectures did not do the trick. During the wrap-up portion of the class, the woman noted that she had enjoyed the workshop but that she was disappointed because I had given few absolutes.

Not to be outdone, I went into a long discussion of absolutes and the flexibility of language and style. It went something like this:

Good editors are not obsessed with commas, spacing around headings, or parallelism. We are obsessed with readers and their ability to understand printed words and thoughts as effortlessly as possible. We advocate clarity, consistency, correctness, conciseness, and other tangibles—some of which do not even begin with "c." That obsession compels us to weed out wordy constructions, untangle convoluted sentences, unpack noun strings, and the like. We do these things even before we know what to call them; we seem instinctively to know that readers will not be best served by certain constructions, phrasing, and word choices. That instinct is guided by a feel for the language, the precision of one word over another, and the tones and hues provided by various choices. This "talent" should be continuously improved and strengthened. The instinct cannot be bought, taught, traded, or willed, but it can be enhanced. It does not take well to absolutes. It thrives on diversity and choice, within the confines of a given discipline or stylistic framework.

The answer does not exist in matters of style and preference (by definition). There are many ways of accomplishing the editor's goal—clear, concise, consistent, correct communication. In training new editors and evaluating new and experienced ones, supervisors frequently make the mistake of insisting on adherence to *their* preferences or the ways that *they* would handle the sentence. The implication is that the editor being evaluated has handled a problem incorrectly, not simply differently. Personal and style preferences should not be stated as absolutes; they allow choices. We are generally taught to prefer the active voice over the passive, but not necessarily to choose it. Therefore, the use of the passive voice is not absolutely incorrect. However, if we encounter a singular verb with a plural subject, a discussion of absolutes is in order; that is, "they is" is always incorrect. That is a point of grammar and is an absolute.

Remember, editors are the readers' advocates. As such, we search for words, phrases, and stylistic techniques that allow readers to understand exactly, not partially, what the author intended. Editing is not an exact science; it is an art guided by instinct and enhanced by training and the tools of the trade.

So, will I bend, go against all my principles, and endorse *the answer* (otherwise called "my personal preference")? Absolutely not.

The Perfection Trap

Striving for perfection... is both neurotic and futile
—Edwin Bliss

As editors we make our living by being conscientious, but we must be careful to distinguish between good work and perfection or we'll get bogged down in minutiae. Perfectionism saps energy, steals time, and eventually stands between you and career advancement. Here are some ways to conquer perfectionist tendencies:

▲ *Ask why.* Determine the reasons behind your drive for perfectionism; are the reasons valid?

▲ *Set realistic limits.* If your "to do" list is mile-high, cut it down to size by focusing on the three most important items on the list.

▲ *Assign priorities to all tasks.* Distinguish between high- and low-priority projects and spend your time accordingly.

by *Elizabeth L. Reed*

Technical Editors: Please Apply!

You don't have to be a "techie" to fill this growing editorial niche

A technical editor does not need to be an engineer, chemist, or physicist to be a good editor in these fields. What are required are basic editorial skills, a systematic approach, and a willingness to learn.

Scientific writing places a high value on precision; the leaner the prose the better. Editors who are able to combine a strong lay interest in the hard sciences and who have a predisposition for clarity, conciseness, and consistency as part of their personal editorial styles can become successful technical editors.

Beginning at the Beginning

The neophyte technical editor should begin developing a familiarity with one or two specific scientific disciplines through proofreading; wise supervising editors assign such tasks to newcomers to the field. Proofreading serves as a good introduction to the preferred style manual. This is usually a house style book or a manual developed by a professional association for its journals. Proofreading can also introduce the beginning technical editor to some of the idiosyncrasies of scientific style that cut across various disciplines, for example, the range of possibilities in the abbreviations for units of measurement. The proofreader's perch is also a good vantage point from which to observe the preferences of the senior editor and the relationship between the technical staff and the publications department.

When approaching new scientific fields, editors should also seek general information by reading as widely as possible in the lay literature of the field. They should spend as much time as needed looking up definitions of terms in the specialized dictionaries and encyclopedias of the science they are interested in and study technical journals for clues on the accepted styles for presenting data and references.

Next Steps

As familiarity increases, the next stage is simple copyediting. Most organizations need fast and accurate copyeditors who can check for conformity to style, edit citations, and correct grammar and usage. (The rules of subject-verb agreement, punctuation, usage, and spelling apply just as readily when the substance of a paragraph involves polysyllabic enzymes as when common nouns and verbs are providing the meat of the sentences.) Editors with good, basic copyediting skills can also ensure congruity of the document's format, content, and pagination.

At this stage the budding technical editor's best education will come in the "read-behind" process. The beginner should follow along as a senior editor reviews his or her work, absorbing the master's experience. It is particularly useful to learn the areas that senior editors check automatically.

From Learning the Ropes to Meeting Expectations

As familiarity develops into competence, more complex editorial tasks can be undertaken, again under the supervision of a more senior technical editor with a stronger background in the specific scientific area. Once a beginner has enough experience and has acquired the basics of one or several disciplines, he or she is ready to leave the nest and try some substantive editing: writing transitions and introductions, suggesting graphic displays for data, and preparing executive summaries and abstracts.

Along the way, the technical editor will not only have picked up some of the basics of computer science, botany, or aeronautical engineering, but will also have internalized the basic expectations that a technical editor is supposed to meet. Some of the more important ones are the following:

▲ Technical editors are expected to function as part of a team that includes in-house technical experts, the publications staff, and—of course—the author. Getting out a good technical publication is often more of a collaborative effort than other kinds of publications work.

▲ Technical editors have to be especially sensitive to the relationships between tables, figures, graphs, and charts on the one hand and the text on the other. In many (if not most) scientific publications, these displays are not merely illustrative; the bulk of the information is communicated through them, while the text carries the reader from one such "information center" to another.

▲ Along the same line, technical editors must make sure that various figures are self-sufficient, providing all the information needed to understand them.

▲ Technical editors are sometimes called on to improve the text. For example, readers of scientific articles often make calculations from figures, which requires the editor to ensure the accuracy of data points. Call-outs and terms used in figures must match the text.

▲ Technical editors are expected to know how to set up an equation, that is, that it has an equal sign and that parentheses and brackets come in pairs. (Because it is assumed you went to college, it is likewise assumed you know the Greek alphabet, upper and lower case.)

▲ Technical editors are also expected to master the various styles of citations for references, recognize all conventional units of measurement and their abbreviations, and know the International System of Units. They should also have a sense for when converting conventional units is appropriate.

A Full-fledged Tech Editor

Once the beginner has earned his or her stripes, more advanced technical editing will include reorganizing and rewriting material, often entire sections or documents. The advanced editor is able to make different levels of decisions, such as when information would be better presented textually or graphically, which material would be better summarized in the text or placed in an appendix, how tables can be improved by different column headings or a change in the style of presentation, and when to add or delete figures to improve reader understanding.

Experienced technical editors often join the professional societies in the fields in which they edit, as well as such publications societies as the Society for Technical Communication. They take the trouble to attend meetings and seminars that give them the chance to improve their specific skills and to develop professionally as editors. Perhaps most important, they see themselves as a breed apart. They know and understand one another's triumphs and tragedies just a little more keenly than "other" editors do. They are not professional scientists, but they know they don't have to be. They also know the scientists couldn't get along without them.

Policies, Procedures, and People

by Mara T. Adams

Do You Need an Editorial Policy?

*A policy statement can
save an editor's hide*

Yes! Because it's what editors can hide behind when the executive director's sister thinks the magazine needs more "human interest" and submits a story about her cats. Although the definition is partly tongue in cheek, it points to the fact that editorial policy is one thing no publications program should be without—yet it is the one thing most of them lack.

Usually, the rationale for not having an editorial policy is the lack of time to formulate one. Not good enough. The time argument doesn't hold up because once the policy is in place, it saves editors far more time than they spent on creating it. A policy can also save a multitude of explanations, hurt feelings, and dicey situations.

Principles: Objectivity First

The basis for all editorial policy must be objectivity. From it arises the entire decision-making structure of an editorial operation, whether the decision concerns publishing or rejecting a second-rate article, refusing a project that conflicts with the editor's personal beliefs, or deciding how much rewriting constitutes tampering with authorship. The editor's objectivity engenders trust: the author's, the publisher's, the advertisers', and the readers'. When an editor loses objectivity, all decisions—even those on line editing—acquire an emotional and thus unprofessional veneer. The mantle of detachment is essential to making decisions that may be controversial. Strongly agreeing or disagreeing with, or strongly liking or disliking, an author is beside the point and will impair editorial judgment. Readers depend on an

27

editor to exercise that judgment in their interests, not as a matter of personal preference. The credible editor must be above personalities and partisanship.

Second, a clearly defined, written statement of what will or won't be published not only protects the editor (and the author's feelings) when a rejection is in order; it also helps to ensure that the publication accepts only what meets its needs. For example, the policy may declare that only serious, substantive articles about the state of the industry, trade, or profession will be entertained and that products and services may be mentioned only in that context. Such a policy will protect the publications program from puff pieces or product releases that advertisers may wish to see in print as a *quid pro quo* for their continued business.

Third, establishing and publishing the criteria for judging the merits of submissions adds to the publishing program's credibility. Such forthrightness also cuts down on inappropriate submissions. Although an editor's "seat of the pants" judgment may be impeccable, it is the editorial policy that makes the judgment stick. To make standards clear, the following benchmarks may be useful:

▲ *Information.* Does the piece deliver the facts promised? Are opinions supported by hard data?

▲ *Analysis.* Are facts examined and woven into an original body of information? Is one fact connected to another?

▲ *Balance.* Are opinions distinguished from facts? Is more than one side of an issue presented?

▲ *Originality.* Does the author bring a fresh perspective to the topic?

▲ *Appeal.* Does the piece address its audience honestly? Does it invite and sustain interest? Is it logical and persuasive?

▲ *Relevance.* Does the piece say something worth saying? Is it timely? Does it challenge or reward the reader?

▲ *Truth.* Do the facts check out? Is the author or the publication responsible for factual accuracy?

Fourth, establishing guidelines on style and format saves wear and tear on copyeditors. Having such a guide means that style decisions need to be made only once, thus avoiding endless rehashing when new copyeditors are hired and manuscripts from new authors are accepted. Once established style guidelines have been communicated to and accepted by frequent contributors, those writers will be grateful that their own work has been made easier. The key words here are *accepted by*. Demonstrating to those in authority that a house style saves time and money in the end also goes a long way toward developing support for a full-blown editorial policy. The secret is for editors to communicate to higher-ups what they know: that many a rewrite has been accepted and many an ego soothed with the words "it's just a matter of our house style." It is then only a short step to the complete editorial policy, which, like the house style, solves problems in advance.

Compromise

If objectivity is the engine of editorial policy and publishing criteria are its pistons, then compromise is surely its lubricant. Indeed, without an editorial policy, there is no room for compromise, precisely because there is nothing that establishes the boundaries within which negotiation can occur.

The concept of levels of edit, for example, is based on the trade-offs that editors must continually make about time, effort, and cost. Levels of edit come into being as editors strive to strike a balance between two facts of publishing life: (1) there are some items that cannot be compromised, and (2) not every manuscript needs or deserves the same degree of editorial attention.

Compromise is not a dirty word; indeed, it is often the magic word in expediting key elements of good editorial work—a workable production schedule, articles that meet deadlines, and a minimum of review cycles and late changes, to name a few. Although there may be times when compromise conflicts with objectivity, lumping compromise under the label of "politics" and pretending to rise above it is not only naive but foolish. Most grown-ups know that mutual back-scratching is the way things get done. The wise and flexible editor knows that the reader can be served in many ways and that some compromises are well worth the trade-off. The place to draw the line is where the result would be a net loss to the reader in clarity, tone, or attractiveness.

Editors exist, after all, to serve readers—to help bring them the message in its clearest, most persuasive, most useful form. To the extent that editorial policies—and editorial compromise—further that end, they should be articulated, defended, and fought for.

by Mara T. Adams

Make the Editorial Board Work for You

A well-chosen board strengthens a publication and supports the editor

The mascot of the editorial review board should probably be the Walrus, that wonderful character in *Through the Looking Glass* who wanted "to speak of many things/Of ships and shoes and sealing wax...And whether pigs have wings."

The image of the editorial board as a body that bogs down in trivia and never reaches a clear consensus is, unfortunately, often accurate.

Editorial boards do have wide-ranging responsibilities, from giving a scholarly journal the right intellectual cachet to steering a true editorial course. A well-chosen board can both strengthen a publication and support its editor. Working with an editorial board is not the same as editing by committee—an unsatisfying and potentially disastrous situation. Rather, the editorial board provides the editor a forum in which to debate ideas, structure content, and refine language.

In some instances, usually scholarly and scientific journals, the editorial board consists of subject specialists who determine acceptability of submissions. In their roles as peer reviewers, the board members serve as resources for the editor and protect the periodical from publishing inferior research. The editor, who is usually a publications expert rather than a subject expert, then has full authority over the number and kinds of editorial changes necessary to make accepted manuscripts presentable to the journal's audience.

In other cases, the editor controls content and the editorial board acts as a kind of Greek chorus, commenting on the substance and the expression of the various articles. The editor then gathers all the written comments, incorporating the best and most relevant and ignoring the rest. This exercise can be particularly interesting: Each member of the board will tend to focus on a different aspect of an article or an entire issue, often forcing the editor to see it from a new and perhaps clearer point of view. It can also be time-consuming, requiring one or more additional cycles in the review process.

There is, of course, a delicate balance between the value of a variety of perspectives and the potential for a truly sour broth. The members of the editorial board should therefore be chosen with extreme care. One of the editorial board's most valuable functions is to protect the editor from acute tunnel vision. Obviously, in any such bouillabaisse, one person must clearly be the final authority on all matters of content and style. Ideally, this person is the editor, although, for political or other reasons, someone else may be the arbiter.

The relationship between the editor and the editorial board need not be adversarial. The board members should be included in planning meetings when articles for the coming year are brainstormed and decided. Soliciting board members' ideas and suggestions at this point in the process not only helps the editor shape the periodical for the year but also gives the board a stake in the product and precludes dissension further down the road. The interaction between the editor and the board is, at its best, a lively intellectual exchange that benefits both the participants and the periodical.

by Bruce O. Boston

Writers Need Guidance

Tell writers what you expect of them before they begin

E ditors who receive queries and freelance submissions, who assign articles to staff or to organization members, or who are obliged to print submissions from board members need more than garden-variety help. A set of "Writers' Guidelines" specifying your requirements can eliminate unwanted editorial correspondence and save your editorial staff much time in manuscript preparation. For example, it's just as easy for writers to triple-space copy if you tend to do a lot of interlinear correction and rewriting in house. Telling writers exactly the form you want the manuscript in can avoid all that crabbed writing in the margins and paper-clipped sheets of emendations that inevitably get lost.

Try to keep guidelines to one page, either both sides of an 8-1/2" x 11" sheet or a two-fold, 11" x 17" sheet that can fit into a standard number 10 envelope. If you want, spruce up your guidelines a bit by printing them on colored stock or use colored ink (not red) on white or off-white paper. Your tone should be authoritative. The assumption is you are communicating with professionals; competent writers will respect and abide by your wishes.

A good set of writers' guidelines should contain the following elements at a minimum:

▲ *Queries*—what you want to know from writers who seek an assignment from you, for example, an article's basic idea, an outline, a statement on why the article will appeal to your readers or meet their needs, the proposed length of the article, and the qualifications of the writer. Unless you don't mind receiving phone calls, state clearly that you will accept no telephone queries.

▲ *Editorial perspective*—a brief statement on what need your publication meets and the kinds of articles your readers are interested in. Mention the titles of some recent articles you've published or briefly describe one or two typical ones. Some editors also make clear the kind of submissions they will not buy, for example, "no poetry or first-person."

▲ *Audience*—a profile of who your readers are, the size of your publication's circulation, and what your readers depend on your publication for.

▲ *Manuscript and diskette preparation*—size of paper, margins, spacing, whether you accept photocopies or dot matrix printouts; your general editorial style (Chicago, GPO, APA, or house), and your style for footnotes and bibliography. If you follow a house style, it is not fair to ask outsiders to conform to it. Usually only professional journals require submissions in a specific style, such as Chicago. If you prefer to receive computer disks from authors, state the size of diskette, type of computer system, and the type(s) of word processing program your office can accept. State whether authors should code manuscript files for boldface, italic, indents, centering, and other formatting options. And specify whether you require a printout of the manuscript in addition to a computer file.

▲ *Electronic submissions*—your specifications and instructions for accepting manuscripts via modem transmission.

▲ *Review procedures*—whether in-house, peer review, or some combination of the two, how long it takes you to report back to writers, and how much time usually elapses between submission and publication.

▲ *Photos*—specifications for size, whether you use color, whether you pay additional fees for photos submitted with articles, and how much.

▲ *Copyright understanding*—a clear statement of exactly what rights you buy and what rights can be negotiated. Reprint rights and availability of reprints should also be stated.

▲ *Payment*—the rates your publication pays for different kinds of submissions and when you pay (on acceptance or on publication). Publications pay in copies, per word, per column-inch, or on a flat-fee basis. Some publications reimburse writers' expenses. Be clear and specific. Usually a range is given and writers know to expect payment on the low end until they prove themselves. Don't pay less than your bottom figure. If you don't pay in cash, the very least you can do is provide copies of the issue in which the writer's article appeared; some publications offer a free year's subscription in lieu of cash.

The most common complaint of editors is inappropriate submissions. The writer is usually at fault; it happens because he or she has not bothered to research your publication, read it, and get some idea of who the audience is and what you are interested in seeing. Above all, your guidelines should encourage writers to read your publication and study it. Writers' guidelines will save you and the writers time, and no one has enough of that.

Tips for Working with Volunteer Reporters

Stringers are what you make of them

Company and other in-house newsletters depend largely on paid employees, not on the publications staff to find and report on interesting stories. Keeping together a staff of dependable stringers is not easy, but you can turn a cadre of reporters from a headache into a real asset by following a few simple procedures:

▲ Cultivate people you can count on for each aspect or department of the newsletter.

▲ Design a news-gathering form for reporters. It should require such things as a statement of the story's main idea, the five Ws and an H (who, what, where, when, why, and how), and reminders about spelling people's names correctly.

▲ Develop a simple reporter's handbook outlining procedures, giving tips, and providing all necessary information. It will cut down on your own follow-up time as well as on rewriting.

▲ Take a reporter to lunch—or better yet, put on an annual recognition luncheon. Include top company brass and a guest speaker.

▲ Give bylines. Nothing beats the thrill of seeing your name in print.

▲ Follow up regularly. Call your reporters to see what they need and to tell them what you need from them.

Questions to Clarify
Writing Assignments

*Editors can help writers prepare better
stories by answering these questions*

People who don't write for a living have an irritating habit of diminishing the effort required to produce a good manuscript. When your supervisor casually requests that the publications department "put together a few words about such and such," what he or she may really have in mind is an in-depth report that requires extensive research. To clarify the assignment and avoid frustration among your writers, get answers to the following questions during the initial conversation about the work:

▲ Who is the audience? How will the manuscript be used—in an employee publication or for placement in the national press?

▲ What is the goal? Will the piece be used to sell a product or service, to enhance the prestige and visibility of the company, or to educate the audience about a current situation in the industry? If there is more than one priority, ask your supervisor to rank them.

▲ Are there special problems associated with the topic? Is this a politically sensitive issue? Is there a hidden agenda?

▲ What past actions or decisions affect the situation your authors will write about?

▲ What resources will be available? Has the topic been covered before? Are the articles available or must your authors find them? Will other staff members be available to do research? Will professional sources inside your company and in the industry be available for interviews?

▲ What is the project's deadline and what priority does your supervisor give the project in relation to your department's existing workload?

▲ How often and at what points does your supervisor want you to check with him or her concerning this project? Aside from your supervisor, who else will review the manuscript?

—Test Yourself—

Words for measurements

What do the following units measure?

1. lumen	5. roentgen	9. erg
2. maxwell	6. volt	10. angstrom
3. gauss	7. hertz	11. kelvin
4. ohm	8. farad	12. stoke

Answers on p. 96.

by Mara T. Adams

Plugging Editorial Holes

A back-up file may one day stand between you and an editorial abyss

How does a newsletter (or any other) editor create a backlog of interesting articles?

▲ *Read the current literature in the field.* Keeping abreast of new developments—whether in desktop publishing, laser printing and scanning, or publishing software—enables you to keep track of trends, to identify creative voices who have something to say, and to get the jump on the competition by publishing new ideas as they develop. You must be willing to take some risks, but the reward is to be identified as a trend-setter.

▲ *Cultivate relationships with industry movers and shakers.* Nurturing such relationships can give you a view of the field that others, who seldom have the luxury of becoming generalists, cannot acquire. By talking to the people who know, and then faithfully reporting the results, you can help some readers make reasoned decisions instead of hasty ones.

▲ *Scan the competition for interesting tidbits.* This is a lazy person's tactic, but it still has its useful aspects. Not all readers have the time or the inclination to read every periodical in their field, and newsletter editors can perform a real service by offering a digest of new information.

▲ *Assign more material than you need for each issue.* If all goes according to plan, the surfeit of manuscripts will soon have your files bulging with articles competing for space on the printed page. If not, at least there should be enough to fill that last half page.

▲ *Keep a commonplace book.* The wise editor (synonymous with the well-prepared editor) keeps such a book or a file of article ideas that can be turned into an article on short notice if the lead contributor runs off with a carhop and leaves no forwarding address.

▲ *Make use of the resources at hand.* Seeing the potential in a staff person previously unthought-of as a contributor sets the visionary editor apart from the pedestrian one. The clerical staff in a publishing house may have a fresh perspective on what it takes to prepare a manuscript for publication.

Of course, building and maintaining a file of back-up articles for a periodical requires constant thought, research, and vigilance. Most editors do not have the time or are too preoccupied with deadlines to become ruminants. Failing all else, you yourself can contribute that luminosity of thought, that clarity of vision, that literacy of expression which will satisfy both the reader's thirst for information and the editor's need for respite.

by Mara T. Adams

Setting Editorial Productivity Standards

Guidelines help editors gauge performance, plot schedules, and project costs

Of all the issues facing publications managers, devising and enforcing productivity standards are among the thorniest. Estimates of time and cost, essential for the proper management and smooth functioning of a publications program, must have a realistic and empirical basis. Setting standards of productivity, vital though they are, often appears to be an exercise in futility because of the elusive nature of the work editors do.

In an assembly-line operation, measuring productivity is easy—you just count the number of widgets Person A produced and compare that with the outputs of Persons B and C. But how many cover designs should a graphic designer produce in a day? How long should it take to write an annual report? How fast can you edit the president's speech? Intellectual and creative output do not submit readily to quantification. Yet, with no productivity standards, there is no basis for evaluating the performance and effectiveness of workers. In publications work, measuring productivity is easier said than done, but it is possible.

Knowns and Unknowns

You may know, for example, that a team of proofreaders working at top speed can get through 15 double-spaced pages per hour and that a single proofreader can do 11 pages per hour. From this base you can establish an acceptable range of pages per hour—say, 12 to 15 for the team, and 9 to 12 for the single proofer—with one error per 10 double-spaced pages as an acceptable error rate. Having ranges such as these is essential in estimating how long a job will

41

take. And, when you're working against a short deadline, the ability to estimate accurately may be crucial.

But in setting productivity standards, you must also allow for variables that you cannot know. You may not know, for example, whether the manuscript against which galleys are being proofed has been edited. If it has not, proofreaders may find a zillion inconsistencies to query. You may not know how good a job the typesetter will do in arranging the letterspacing and leading, or in setting figure captions and table titles, when you are estimating how long pasteup should take. You may not know whether the manuscript you are holding has been produced by a good writer or a hack—or, even if produced by a good writer, whether it is clean and relatively free of typos.

Often, the deadline will set productivity standards for you. Your standards will be based on the volume of work to be completed and the amount of time available.

Before devising productivity standards, observe your staff at work. Monitor not only their output, but their work habits and patterns as well. The results of these observations will give you a clearer picture of whether you are getting the most from your workers already, need more staff, or need to make changes in assignments. You may, in fact, be getting the best from your staff because they feel comfortable; if you make additional demands on them, quality may suffer.

Quantity and Quality

When you establish productivity standards, strike a balance between quantity and quality. Quality, after all, is what publications managers have to sell. Indeed, in an environment that puts a low value on the editorial function, quality may be the *only* element standing between your department and the unemployment line.

Productivity thus not only means putting out a volume of work; it means getting out a volume of *acceptable* work. To get good performance, a manager has to ask for it and expect it. Nor is asking as difficult as it seems. Most people want to do a good job and take satisfaction from the work itself. They respond to high standards with their best performance.

Tools

Virtually every publications task can be committed to a checklist, which can break the job down into measurable chunks, giving a staff member a blueprint for organizing the work. If you fill out a checklist for each project and keep a file copy, you can follow up with honest, written feedback on a worker's performance over a period of time.

Having asked for good performance, you have to reinforce it. A sincere word of praise or thanks can work wonders. Use of a feedback form to record excellent work (as well as work that needs improvement) lets the worker know that there is a permanent record of achievement in the personnel file that should be rewarded come review time.

The key to effective productivity measures is moderation. Idle time is not necessarily unproductive time; allow a degree of flexibility in your expectations. Set an example by meeting all your own deadlines. Offer help when it's needed; distribute the work equitably. Above all, do not use productivity standards as a whip. Such standards are simply guides to help you control the work flow, not a rigid code from which no deviation is permissible.

On the Reference Shelf

The top ten books used by EEI's editors

Although as editors we pride ourselves on our mental retention of countless rules of grammar and style, we also appreciate the importance of reliable professional reference texts. In an informal poll of EEI's editors and writers, the following reference books ranked in the top ten texts that were essential to these publications professionals' work. Here are the top ten:

Webster's Ninth New Collegiate Dictionary
The Chicago Manual of Style, 13th ed.
Words into Type, by Marjorie Skillin and Robert Gay, 3d ed.
American Usage and Style: The Consensus, by Roy H. Copperud
The Careful Writer: A Modern Guide to English Usage, by
    Theodore M. Bernstein
United States Government Printing Office (GPO) Style Manual,
    1984 ed.
Roget's II: The New Thesaurus
Pocket Pal, International Paper Company, 13th ed.
The Elements of Style, by William Strunk and E. B. White
Oxford English Dictionary (OED), 2d ed.

How to Edit Articles
by Specialists

Don't be cowed by "experts"

When you edit manuscripts by specialists, remember that they are not likely to be writers. Yet, you need their contributions, and they need your editorial help.

Recognize that specialists are fact-oriented. They have little sensitivity for the audience and only a rough mastery of words. They pack into an article too many facts, figures, percentages, and citations. They are as likely to include trivial facts as major data. Your job as editor is to select the important, cut the unimportant, and retain only the facts needed to advance the movement of the piece.

Awareness of the Reader

Because specialists are concerned with facts, they are often unaware of the reader's needs and interests. Specialists assume that everyone knows, or should know, what they are talking about and that everyone cares deeply about the topic. Specialists are frequently concerned not with enlightening the reader but with "advancing scholarship" or promoting a point of view.

The editor must protect the reader from specialists' insensitivities or blind spots. Early in the manuscript, write in sentences to show why the material could be important to the reader, how it could be used, and why it should be read.

The Trouble with Openings

Assume almost as a certainty that the opening paragraphs of a specialist's manuscript will be unusable. The lead and the first

45

hundred words will present the biggest challenge in editing a specialist's work.

Specialists fail to see the need for attention-getting openers, often fail to define the topic, and frequently fail to tell the reader where the article is going or what to expect from the material. As the editor, you will have to bridge these gaps for the author—through editing. (An alternative is to send the manuscript back to the author with suggestions. However, when the manuscript comes back, you may find little change.)

Working Through the Prose
Once you have fixed the lead, clarified the article's subject and approach, and indicated its value to the reader, you must cope with a host of language problems.

Specialists' language is usually grammatically correct. For example, the sentence "Completion of the study will be accomplished by the year 1998" is correct, but it is the editor's job to find the real subject and the real verb in sentences of this type. These would be easier to locate if the sentence read "The team will complete the study by 1998."

Don't Be Timid
In editing specialists, don't be intimidated by titles, prestige, or reputation. Go after the convoluted, complex sentences with words ending in -tion, -ation, -ment. These word endings are clues for turning the sentence around, using a real subject and a strong verb, into direct, active, shortened statements. Rewriting such sentences will greatly improve the manuscript.

Other Soft Spots
Be ready to confront other common weaknesses in the specialist's writing. You may find the following:

▲ *Pomposity.* Specialists achieve this by using big words and blowing up simple concepts into presumably complex ones. Deflate pomposity with your editing pencil.

▲ *Repetition.* Scholars and experts have little faith in the reader's ability to grasp content; therefore, they repeat themselves. Cut repetition ruthlessly.

▲ *Zealousness.* Specialists are partisans, either for a special cause or point of view. Such an attitude is acceptable. Unacceptable, however, are overstatements and reiteration of arguments already made.

▲ *Colorful writing.* To sugar-coat copy, specialists, inexplicably, inject whimsy, belabored metaphors, extravagant prose, or jokes. Such efforts, from the hands of the inexpert, become tiresome or distasteful. As a service to the reader, cut them out.

Adapted with permission from the August 1978 issue of Edpress News.

Tips to Improve Copy Flow

Use the "95 percent" rule

Rita Stollman, a partner in Creative Business Concepts, an editorial management consulting firm in Mt. Vernon, NY, cautions her clients to get editorial management involved early in the editing and proofreading phases to avoid costly copy corrections late in the production cycle.

Stollman notes that senior editors often either reject or rewrite articles midway through the editorial cycle, thereby playing havoc with publication schedules and driving up cost. She suggests that the senior editor review manuscripts when they come in and discuss trouble spots and structural problems with the junior editor who will edit or rewrite the text. When the rewrite is complete, the senior and junior editors should review the new draft together. Giving junior editors initial guidance increases the chances of getting a usable manuscript and decreases last-minute changes.

Stollman urges editors to make *all* copy changes before the manuscript goes to typesetting, even if it means building more time into the production cycle. When copy comes back from typesetting or desktop publishing, use the "95 percent rule." If 95 percent of your readers won't notice the missing hyphen on page 25, don't touch it. Correct only misspellings and factual errors at this stage.

by Connie Moy

Editing the Prima Donna

Tips to help editors work with difficult authors

N ancy Davidson has learned what it takes to edit temperamental academics successfully. She is an associate editor at the Brookings Institution, a public policy think-tank in Washington, DC, where many of today's (and tomorrow's) top-level issues are analyzed by some of the brightest people in the world. They don't necessarily take kindly to editing, and that's the point at which Davidson's skills amount to more than the ability to sift out the dangling participles and comma splices.

Ask her to describe her job and she'll tell you it's part editorial skill, part tact, and part teaching ability, with the emphasis decidedly on the latter two. She confesses, "During my interview for the position at Brookings, they were as concerned about my ability to deal with academics as they were with my editing qualifications."

In her editorial career, both as a freelancer and as a staff member at Brookings, Davidson has developed a successful method for working with difficult authors—from the starry-eyed newcomers who believe their every word is a pearl to the full professor who has been known to intimidate a senator or cabinet member.

Getting to Know You

At the outset, Davidson says, it's important to get to know the author. She tries to have a face-to-face conversation with each writer to determine if he or she views the editing process as a necessary nuisance or as a valuable step in making the book or article better. Is the author ready to turn the work over and let her handle every detail? Does the writer want only periodic consultations or full control over every semicolon?

Davidson believes the editor should not be overawed by the author's credentials or reputation. It is important to let the author know (subtly) that the editor, too, is a professional who commands expertise.

Once Davidson has learned as much as possible about the author, she next learns what she can about the context for the author's work. What stage is it in? Is the author still excited with the project, bored with it, or ready to pitch it out the nearest window? Has the piece been through several revisions already? Will more be required?

If she has already glanced through the manuscript, Davidson talks briefly with the author about the "little" points she has noticed: the length of chapters, the way tables have been deployed, the number of footnotes in each chapter, the appearance of the figures. Experience has taught her that a casual conversation on minor points will often elicit remarks from the author that can help her determine how to handle the editing.

Next, Davidson edits a sample chapter or section. She usually chooses something from the middle of the work that is fairly representative of the job as a whole. During this phase, she does a thorough editing job. She will suggest moving a paragraph here, deleting another there, or changing the wording somewhere else. Once again, a talk with the author is appropriate to assess the reaction to the sample edit.

On to the Query Sheet

Once one chapter has been successfully edited, the task of editing the entire manuscript is eased by a tactfully written query sheet, which explains the changes Davidson prefers and how those changes will improve the final product. A query sheet, she advises, stands a much better chance of eliciting a favorable response from the author than a list of peremptory demands or the return of an entire manuscript awash in blue pencil.

At this point, Davidson says, it is surprising how many authors want to argue grammatical issues with her. The author may have a Ph.D. in economics, but chances are he or she knows little about grammar, except, of course, what some eighth-grade English teacher said. Often, about all the author remembers is "never split an infinitive" and "never begin a sentence with the word *and*." But those points are remembered as gospel!

Here Davidson begins a little in-service education of her own, with the aid of books such as Theodore Bernstein's *Miss Thistlebottom's Hobgoblins*, which Davidson calls a "marvelous" usage book that tells writers everything their eighth-grade teachers should have told them. Davidson's pupils soon find out when it's acceptable (indeed, preferable) to split an infinitive, or when what seems to be a dangling participle is actually an absolute construction. Davidson frequently copies a page from *Miss Thistlebottom's Hobgoblins* and sends it along to an author to buttress a point.

What Happens When the Author Balks?
Sometimes, despite the diplomacy, authors still dig in their heels. What then? Says Davidson, it's time for another conversation. She asks her authors, "Please tell me in your own words exactly what you are trying to say." Davidson says it's amazing how a light bulb often will go on in the editor's brain, illuminating clearly the author's intention *and* a solution.

But sometimes this tactic doesn't work. Neither tact nor a fresh look at the material works. Even a page from *Miss Thistlebottom* does not budge the author. No more quibbling about commas; now is the time for serious compromise. At this point the trade-off becomes the editor's most potent ally; here is where it becomes advisable to give ground on a nonparallel construction, for example, in return for a more substantive change.

Davidson has also devised a strategy for persuading authors to use less opaque language. She reminds them that eliminating jargon or changing phraseology will make the book or article more accessible to a wider audience, thus helping to ensure larger sales. Many authors find the argument appealing.

Court of the Last Resort
When all else fails, Davidson's fallback position is to invoke the house style guide, pointing out that it says *not* to capitalize the names of government programs like social security. She points out that another effective strategy can be kicking the problem

upstairs: A managing editor or director of publications can be most helpful to staff editors. But, she admits ruefully, even Brookings has had to give in to a few unyielding authors; even the house style guide can be overridden.

Although few disputes go beyond author and editor, there is a final precept for the editor to remember when dealing with a prima donna: When the last battle over a misplaced modifier has been lost, when all of your efforts toward clarification have been in vain, remember that the work really does belong to the author.

Exercise Sound Editorial Judgment

A skilled editor's judgment goes beyond the rule books

"We live in a society that is driven to a great degree by marketing," observes John B. Campbell, magazine editorial consultant and former editorial director for the Hearst Business Publishing Group. "It is all too easy for those who spend advertising dollars to assume that editors, and the publications they edit, are primarily tools to help them move products."

Campbell urges editors to remember that their first responsibility is to serve readers, not advertisers. Noting that the "real world" of publishing economics sometimes pressures editors and reporters to slant coverage favorably toward advertisers, Campbell points out several areas in which the integrity of editorial content can be threatened.

▲ *Phantom sources.* We've all read quotes that begin, "Industry sources say...." Such statements can be the result of honest reporting, but may be rhetorical tricks used to set off opposing views, or worse, the statements may be fabrications.

▲ *Incomplete reporting.* Sometimes reporters knowingly fail to contact sources whose information or viewpoints go against the main point of the story.

▲ *Oversimplification.* This disservice is the norm in broadcast journalism where reporters must reduce broad, complex issues to "sound bites." There is time for only the black and white; the shades of gray—often the areas in which the truth lies—are ignored.

▲ *Nonexistent trends.* How many reported trends are genuine—supportable through objective, quantified research—and how many emerge because they make for a good story?

▲ *Distorted graphics.* Statistics, and the graphics to illustrate them, can be a minefield of misinterpretation. How often do we tinker slightly with the numbers to create a more sensational graphic and therefore a more dramatic argument?

▲ *Factual errors.* Every publication prints errors occasionally, but how often are they acknowledged and corrected in print? Campbell cites one editor who refused to run corrections for fear that the publication would lose credibility. That editor probably wasn't alone.

Editorial integrity can get lost in the daily rush of deadlines, the pressure to get "good" stories, and the concern for profitability. The loss of editorial integrity can be an insidious process; editors must be sensitive to it if they hope to guard against it.

Adapted from Folio *magazine.*

by Linda Jorgensen

Uphold the Readers' Bill of Rights

The reader is the most important person you work with

A writer's need to communicate and a reader's need to know aren't always the same, according to Washington, DC, author and writing instructor Dianne Snyder. Yet writers often forget this basic principle of their craft and ignore three built-in reader expectations—what Snyder calls a "readers' bill of rights." If a writer fails to meet these expectations, readers become confused and lose interest. Readers have a right to—

▲ A meaningful context for the ideas being presented. (Why bother reading without one? Snyder asks her students.)

▲ A hierarchy of ideas with structural bridges that show how one idea relates to the next. (If one thing doesn't lead to another, why continue reading?)

▲ An early indication of what the text will cover. (Readers like to know what they're getting; "bait and switch" tactics are unfair in writing as well as in commerce.)

Snyder says that writers most often violate this readers' bill of rights because they approach writing differently from the way their audience reads the finished work. For example, writers—

▲ Tend to tell a story, whether fact or fiction, in chronological order, even though the events might be clearer or more effective if presented in a different sequence.

▲ Often assume that their readers' familiarity with a topic approaches their own.

▲ Assume that their point of view is shared by the readers, or that the readers will indulge the writer's speculations without argument.

To avoid losing their readers, Snyder urges writers to review their work from the readers' point of view, making sure that the material—

▲ Presents information in a logical sequence tailored to the readers' knowledge of the subject.

▲ Cues readers on what to expect as the subject is developed so that there is no need to "fill in the gaps."

▲ Considers possible objections, questions, or gaps in expertise that might cause an attentive reader to dismiss the writing.

The Writer's Checklist of Readers' Needs

Snyder provides her writing students with the following checklist of readers' needs to help evaluate whether the readers' bill of rights has been honored.

▲ Have I stated my purpose clearly in the opening paragraph(s)?

▲ Have I let the readers know what to expect from the text?

▲ Have I provided a context for my ideas?

▲ Have I highlighted the main ideas?

▲ Have I told readers everything they need to know?

▲ Have I included anything they don't need to know?

▲ Is the level of language consistent with the readers' backgrounds and familiarity with the subject?

▲ Does the style of presentation serve my underlying purpose of persuading, informing, or moving the readers to action?

▲ Have I anticipated readers' questions about the subject?

▲ Have I anticipated readers' attitudes toward the subject?

▲ Are readers likely to draw inferences that I had not intended?

by Molly Bentsen

Freelancers Can Enliven Your Publication

Follow these suggestions to keep good workers working for you

M any publishers rely heavily on editorial freelancers to help them transform projects from manuscript to printed page. There are concerns and potential problems unique to the publisher-freelancer relationship, but you can make it work and work well.

It is easy to fall into an "out of sight, out of mind" neglect of freelance workers because they don't do their daily work on the premises. But remembering freelancers' interests and meeting their needs can serve both them and you. Training people to do their jobs well is costly, and that is no less true for freelance workers. Cultivating worker stability brings a profitable harvest.

Set the stage for success when you first interact with potential freelance workers:

▲ *Know your needs.* Identify the types of projects best suited to freelancers. Will the work be ongoing or infrequent? Do you need the expertise of a veteran and have the budget to hire one, or are you willing to provide on-the-job training? Finding an experienced person who will work for a song is wishful thinking, but neither should you have to pay top dollar for a novice. To save inquirers' time and yours, outline clearly what you expect and what you can offer.

▲ *Screen candidates properly.* Solicit work samples or administer a test covering the skills your projects will require. Conduct a personal or telephone interview and check references. Whatever the job, look for a solid base of skills as you evaluate prospective freelancers. It's simple enough to correct a freelancer's querying procedures or misinterpretations of style nuances, but a mediocre eye for misspelling and detail or poor organization skills aren't problems you'll want to tackle. You might suggest appropriate books, courses, or other resources to applicants who have good skills but lack the experience to meet your needs; perhaps with some study they'll make suitable candidates.

▲ *Orient new workers.* Introduce new freelancers to your company. If they are local residents, invite them to meet their in-house colleagues. Talk through your publishing process so that newcomers can see how their contributions fit into the whole. Discuss the procedures and standards that apply to their work, and make sure they have the proper resources to do the job you expect. If you use a standard style manual, lend copies to freelancers or sell the manual at a discount. Provide a house style sheet or manual detailing other specific requirements.

Once you've established a working relationship, treat freelancers fairly and give them adequate support.

▲ *Be fair.* Before determining pay rates for freelancers, find out what other companies in your area pay for comparable freelance work; then reevaluate the market periodically. Draw up a contract to specify deadlines and payment details for every project; make deadlines reasonable. From the outset, make your expectations for the quality of work clear, and state your procedures for substandard projects.

▲ *Keep in touch.* Offer in-service training to freelancers to build their skills, and give specific feedback on completed projects. Build bridges of communication and camaraderie between freelance and in-house professionals. Don't forget to inform off-site staff when new policies and procedures affect their work, and try not to leave them in the dark when internal transitions bring a change in their customary work load or contact person. Solicit feedback, too, about ways you or the company might improve procedures or make freelancers' jobs easier.

To keep good people working for you, recognize and try to address the limitations of freelance work.

▲ *Promote professional growth.* Freelancers miss the interaction among in-house staff. Remember that freelancers are professional colleagues and include them in the information pipeline. Send them copies of pertinent articles from professional publications. Pass along information on courses, books, and resources they might not learn of otherwise.

▲ *Offer incentives.* One guideline stands out as a goodwill booster—pay promptly! Beyond that, think of creative ways to encourage good people to keep working for you (particularly if you can't offer top pay). Make freelancers eligible for the same merit raises offered to in-house employees. Give freelancers complimentary copies of books to which they have contributed their talents. Extend fringe benefits as appropriate (employee discounts, access to company equipment, supplies at discount rates, tuition reimbursement for professional development, and so forth).

▲ *Promote a sense of belonging.* Help freelancers feel the importance of the roles they play. Remember to include them when you're publicizing appreciation for employee contributions to projects. If you publish a company newsletter, send copies to freelance staff. Invite freelancers to company social gatherings and staff development functions. Sponsor an occasional Freelancers' Day at the company to give off-site staff a chance to meet one another and their in-house colleagues.

The principles of good management that foster productivity, longevity, and job satisfaction among permanent employees apply to freelance workers as well. Thoughtful investment of company resources in these workers' development will yield personal, professional, and financial rewards.

Quirks

Why, if there's a who and whom,
Must I ask for you, not youm?
Night by night I've turned and tossed:
How come lose goes not to lossed?
We say "give," in past, "we gave."
We say "live," but can't say "lave."
The joke's the thing that makes a jokester,
But yolks of hen make her no yolkster.
I grow and grow, and say "I grew."
I glow and glow, but never "glew."
On the subject of swim and swam,
If there's a skim, how come no skam?
I do now sit and I had sat.
My clothes now fit, but had not fat.
Who made up these mad requirements,
Causing me to make inquirements?
Why, when checking dictionary,
Are words I want so fictionary?

—*Morris A. Nunes*

by Molly Bentsen

Choosing Between Freelance and Full-time Staff

Each arrangement has its pluses and minuses

C ircumstances unique to each company make this choice a difficult task, but editorial managers should consider the following points before making a decision between using freelancers or full-time staff. You'll need to reevaluate procedures as your organization grows or your editorial needs change.

Freelancer Pluses

▲ The biggest motivator for hiring freelancers is that you use services only as you need them, without the added overhead and other considerations of permanent positions.

▲ The talent pool for your work load enlarges.

▲ A fluctuating work flow is easier to handle because several projects can be completed simultaneously.

▲ Freelancers who work for other companies can offer a fresh perspective and wider networking possibilities than full-time staff.

In-House Pluses

▲ Testing and training time is spent more efficiently.

▲ The in-house employee is available no matter when a project comes in; you needn't compete with a freelancer's other clients for the worker's time or loyalties.

▲ Communication may be clearer because co-workers on a project can talk face-to-face with each other and with the project supervisor.

61

▲ The in-house worker can become familiar with company procedures more quickly, and confusion among varying styles is less
of a problem.

Sweet Rejection

Take the pain out of saying "no"

No writer likes rejection letters, and no conscientious editor
relishes writing them. Joanne Dufilho, of *Mother Earth News*, suggests an unusual way to take the sting out of rejection with this
eloquent letter from the editors of a Chinese economics journal.

> *We have read your manuscript with boundless delight. If we
> were to publish your paper it would be impossible for us to
> publish any work of a lower standard. And as it is unthinkable
> that, in the next thousand years, we shall see its equal, we
> are, to our regret, compelled to return your divine composi-
> tion, and to beg you a thousand times to overlook our short
> sight and timidity.*

Levels and Types
of Editing

by Mary J. Scroggins

Edit for Consistency

Adding editorial polish encourages readers to continue reading

One of the words that I use most frequently when talking and writing about editing or conducting editing or writing workshops is *consistency*. For me, editing and consistency are inevitably connected. Editing clarifies the language, making it more concise, correct, clear, and consistent; consistency provides logical connections between the ideas and parts of any thoughtfully written and edited manuscript.

The English language is rich in stylistic and grammatical variations and choices. Consistency dictates that this richness not clutter a piece (and thus interfere with correct communication) by giving the readers an overabundance of choices.

Readers ought to be able to depend on consistency in editorial style, usage, and format for guidance to the writer's intentions and interpretations. Consistency can hold together a less-than-superior piece that has substance, and it can add polish to a really fine piece. However, imposing a consistent style and format on a poorly written piece with little substance will not make it worth reading even if the piece becomes more tolerable.

Consistency dictates not that the writer or the editor make a *specific* choice of one capitalization scheme over another (for example, "the Institute" rather than "the institute" when referring to an institute previously mentioned by its full name), one plural form over another, one hyphenation pattern over another, or one style over another, but instead that the writer or the editor make a choice (either "the Institute" or "the institute") and stick to it. The writer or editor who fails to make choices, in effect, tells the readers, "I have given you several choices. You make the decisions. I am too careless, too lazy, or too unskilled to handle the abundance of choices." Inconsistency then flourishes, frustrates the readers, and undermines the effectiveness of the manuscript and the credibility of the writer or the project's sponsor. The work is devalued.

Inconsistencies can damage and even destroy credibility. For example, readers are often confused by inconsistencies in hyphenation, such as "two signal analyzers" vs. "two-signal analyzers." Hyphenation is used to avoid confusion and ambiguity and chiefly to establish or clarify relationships between words. If hyphenation is inconsistent or haphazard, readers must guess at relationships. They might logically assume that the writer or project's sponsor is unsure of the relationship or does not care whether the readers understand the relationships. If the writer or editor does not take pains with such obvious matters as hyphenation, number style, spelling preference, capitalization, and abbreviations, how can readers be sure that appropriate care was taken with less obvious details such as accuracy of data collected and thoroughness of research? Inconsistency hangs about such a piece of writing like a sign that warns, "Reader Beware."

Inconsistency may also divert from the writer's purpose. In the struggle to decipher the puzzle of choices, readers may misinterpret, overlook, or completely ignore important information. If readers must decide whether "site," "facility," and "center" refer to the same location or whether the variable on page 2 is the same as the one on page 10, even though one has a capital *C* and the other has a lowercase *c*, energy that should be used to absorb information must be used to consider the probability of intent.

Clearly, consistency should be imposed by the writer and the editor, never the readers. Consistency indicates the writer's and the editor's common respect for the readers and concern for the importance of correct, expedient communication.

Titles and topics invite readers to read; consistency encourages them to continue to read and allows them to understand the message with as little effort as possible. Consistency is the glue that binds the parts without question of interpretation or confusion.

©1988 Mary J. Scroggins

by Marjorie Manwaring

Use the Sweep Strategy

Several editing sweeps ensure a higher "catch" rate

Not satisfied with the way you handled your last editing job? Perhaps your "sweep strategy"—your plan of attack for reading through and editing the manuscript—wasn't efficient.

You perform a sweep, or pass, each time you thumb through all or a portion of a manuscript, whether or not you actually make changes in it. Here is what you can do on different sweeps:

▲ Gain a general familiarity with the manuscript.

▲ Establish the baseline edit.

▲ Identify potential problem areas such as tables, charts, graphs, punctuation, or footnotes.

▲ Check for consistency with previous changes.

▲ Isolate particularly troublesome sections.

▲ Put the manuscript through spelling and grammar checkers on your word processor.

▲ Review the entire manuscript for queries.

Each sweep should be tailored to the manuscript at hand. A successful strategist takes into account the level of edit chosen, the time available, the length of the manuscript, its content and condition, and the editor's individual preferences.

For example, suppose you must edit a long, complex manuscript. Perhaps on your last job you fixed large-scale problems such as organization first and more specific problems such as style and grammar later. This time, however, it might be more efficient to perform smaller scale sweeps first so you can become more familiar with the content. You can then perform larger scale emendations more confidently and effectively.

Similarly, if you don't have time to read the entire manuscript carefully, adopting the correct sequence of sweeps can raise the quality of the finished product or decrease the editing time required, or both.

Once you've devised a strategy, you may have to modify it; what you learn and do using one strategy might require you to alter later sweeps. Revised deadlines and schedules will also affect strategies.

Planning your overall strategy takes some headwork. But making well-thought-out decisions about the number and type of sweeps you'll perform can improve the quality of your work and your efficiency as an editor. The extra effort will quickly become well worth your while.

This article is adapted from the book How to Teach Technical Editing, *written by David Farkas and published by the Society for Technical Communication.*

by Priscilla S. Taylor

Minimal Editing: How Much Is Too Much?

Sometimes "once over lightly" is all an editor is allowed to do

How should an editor handle a bylined article by a well-known author? Use "minimal editing," says the U.S. Census Bureau's Gerald A. Mann. Mann gave these suggestions for such editing at the 27th International Technical Communications Conference of the Society for Technical Communication in 1980:

▲ Correct mechanical errors, but don't change the author's style unless it interferes with readability.

▲ Review the entire manuscript for proper reader "framing" and focus, usually through a good introduction and appropriate writing style.

▲ Check for a clear plan of organization, with good transition from section to section.

▲ Try to ensure that no questions will be unanswered in the reader's mind.

▲ Make only those changes that can be justified in terms of the reader's needs: don't allow your personal preferences to intrude on the author's style.

An example of minimal editing is shown in the box below. Mann comments, "The edited version retains the style and tone of the original, but includes some minor rephrasing to clarify the meaning. Nothing that remains in the edited version of this passage is incorrect; it is simply more ornate than many of us are accustomed to."

Mann continues, "An inexperienced editor might have practically rewritten the entire passage with an eye to achieving a low Fog count, but in doing so he or she would have completely eliminated the author's distinctive style. Not only would this be presumptuous and unfair to the author, it would be unjustified in terms of the reader's needs. The typical reader interested in this kind of subject matter will also probably appreciate this kind of style."

Original version

To represent in painting the joining of the two worlds in forms which are, as it were, true to nature, is necessarily one of the most difficult and challenging tasks of art. It involves a paradox: the artist has to represent the invisibility of the gods, or their transition from invisibility to epiphany, in a visual medium and yet he has to make it look—as, indeed, must be the case when it happens in nature—as if this transition were one of the most natural occurrences that connect heaven and earth. The gods in the woods and the fields are the spirits of the landscape and, as such, have a life and will of their own, but they are also the landscape itself, or its real sense, and must therefore, if adequately rendered, in all of their manifestations be recognizable in the duplicity of their uniqueness.

Minimally edited version

To represent in painting the joining of the two worlds, in a form which is true to the nature of each, is necessarily one of the most difficult and challenging tasks of art. It involves a paradox: The artist must represent the invisibility of the gods, or their transition from invisibility to epiphany, in a visual medium, and he also has to make it look as if this transition were one of the most natural occurrences that connect heaven and earth. The gods in the woods and fields are the spirits of the landscape with a life and will of their own, but they are also the landscape itself, or its real sense; their adequate rendition, therefore, must clearly represent this unique double nature.

Emergency Surgery: Performing a Crash Edit

How to conquer a manuscript whose deadline looms

One person's interesting—and controversial—opinions on how to edit a manuscript quickly to meet a short deadline are outlined in "Coping with Crash Editing," a talk presented by Brian Jarman at the Society for Technical Communication's 27th International Technical Communications Conference in 1980.

A typical crash editing job, says Jarman, consists of three main steps: psyching up for the job, attacking the manuscript, and deciding how to compromise quality to meet the deadline. Here are Jarman's methods:

Psyching Up
In the first step, psyching up, you develop the right attitude to do the job. Some of the psychological tricks Jarman uses: Cultivate a low, calm voice and a relaxed manner. Establish your control over the job by taking the manuscript from the author as soon as possible. Give an up-tight author your full attention. Hold the manuscript in your hands. Flip through the pages, and ask the author five crucial questions:

▲ What is the manuscript supposed to sell; what is its purpose?

▲ Who will read it?

▲ Is there anything special to be done; for example, are there points to emphasize or to play down?

▲ How far along are the illustrations?

▲ What is the deadline?

71

If the author does not give a definite answer to the last question, get the information you need to figure out the deadline yourself. (For example, will the manuscript be reviewed? If so, when? How many keyboard operators will be available to incorporate editing changes?) Then estimate the time available for editing; do not, at this time, estimate how long it will take to edit the manuscript.

Attacking the Manuscript

Never tell the author the extent or depth of the editing you will do (one of Jarman's controversial statements). Do not read the manuscript; instead, begin to edit (another controversial statement). Determine the level of editing you can do in the time available: Time yourself as you do a full, in-depth editing job at your best speed on the first two pages of text and apply the resulting average rate of speed per page to calculate the time needed for the whole manuscript. Then, if you find you cannot meet the deadline with an in-depth job, edit to a lower level.

As you work, you will set a rhythm. To avoid breaking the rhythm, work as long as you can at a stretch. Edit the text, figures, and tables separately, each to its own rhythm. Go back and read the text to check the descriptions of the figures after you finish editing the figures. Do the same for the tables. Take a few minutes' break to clear your mind. Then read the manuscript, but do not rewrite or edit again; just look for inconsistencies you can correct in a hurry.

Compromising on the Quality of Editing

Following Jarman's assignment of priorities to five levels of editing (as shown in the chart below), edit to the highest priority the available time allows.

Priority	Editing Level (Cumulative)
1	Correct errors in punctuation, grammar, and spelling
2	Make sentences more effective
3	Correct improper word usage
4	Make formatting changes
5	Reorganize contents

(The assignment of priorities is another point of controversy; some editors would change priority 5 to priority 1.)

Jarman says that punctuation is the easiest and quickest way to improve the comprehension of the meaning and grammatical relationship of the author's words. He believes that corrections to grammatical errors and to misspelled words strengthen the credibility of the author's technical voice. These two kinds of editing go hand in hand, and Jarman applies them automatically. They form the foundation of his crash editing, and, for him, all other forms of editing are additive.

The Conscientious Copyeditor at Work

How a copyeditor might have revised history

...~~whose~~ *the* broad stripes and bright stars *of which* through the perilous fight...

—*Francis Scott Key*

The wages of sin ~~is~~ *are* death.

For thine ~~is~~ *are* the kingdom⌿ and the power⌿ and the glory.

—*King James Bible*

The tumult and the shouting dies.

—*Rudyard Kipling*

To be⌿ or not to be: ~~that is~~ *there are* the question *↓*...

And damn'd be ~~him that~~ *he who* first cries, "Hold, enough!"

—*William Shakespeare*

These are the times that try men's *and women's* souls.

—*Thomas Paine*

~~Four score and~~ *Eighty-* seven years ago...

—*Abraham Lincoln*

When ~~in the course of human events it becomes necessary for~~ one people *need* to dissolve the political bands ~~which~~ *that* have connected them...

—*Thomas Jefferson*

by Peggy Smith

I Never Said That!

When can an editor safely tamper with a quotation?

"This journalist, like most, feels it's a cardinal sin to tamper with a quote, even if the effect is to turn it into correct English," Bob Levey, columnist for *The Washington Post*, once wrote. "Honesty is my policy—because it's the best policy."

Levey was justifying his use of uncorrected quotations from a letter writer who had written about "the confusion of my mother and I" and from a telephone caller who had referred to women as "girls."

Is Levey's kind of honesty the best policy for all circumstances? The answer often depends on whether the quotation is from a written source or a spoken source. And the answer can vary with different authorities, publications, and quoters.

Quotes from Written Sources

Responsible writers and editors know they must be sure that quotations repeat an original written source nearly word for word and letter for letter (with omissions and interpolations clearly indicated).

Different authorities specify different style rules on what and how changes can be made. The principle behind any codified style, however, is the same: to be clear and grammatical within the context while being fair to the source.

Some style guides more than others assume that the reader understands that certain small changes may be made without notice.

Such changes include capitalizing or lowercasing an initial letter to fit the context.

Few style guides, however, permit correction of errors. Chicago style permits correction of obvious typos without notice in quoting from a modern document but calls for retention of "any idiosyncrasy of spelling" in quoting from an older work. Other style guides specify that either the suggested correction or the word *sic* be put in brackets after an error.

But style rules are not the same as the courtesy rules that apply to letters to the editor. Some publications post notice; for example, *Time* magazine says, "Letters may be edited for purposes of clarity or space." *The Washington Post* warns, "Because of space limitations, [letters] published are subject to abridgment."

Some publications routinely correct blatant errors without notice but check with the letter writer before making extensive changes. *The New York Times* policy, for example, is to correct misspellings and grammatical errors in letters to the editor, and to make small cuts and changes to fit a letter into the allotted space. If any change of substance is involved, the letter writer is asked to make the cuts.

And *Writer's Digest* usually corrects misspellings and grammatical errors in letters to the editor, unless the errors are intentional (for example, to make fun of something the magazine has done). If time allows, a letter edited for clarity or space is sent to the writer in typeset form before publication.

Quotes from Speakers
On repairing the redundancy, vagueness, jargon, and clichés in interviews, Mel Mandell, former editor of *Computer Decisions*, once wrote, "My remedy and the one I train my editors to apply is heavy editing of quotes.... We never get any complaints."

Lyle L. Erb writes the following on newspaper reporting:

A direct quote should be the speaker's own words. But don't quote illiteracies except where color is needed. It may subject the speaker to ridicule. The speaker will insist it's a misquotation. Correct the grammar and other errors.

According to the Associated Press and United Press International style guides, in writing the news, a reporter should correct errors that "would go unnoticed in speaking, but are embarrassing in print." The official reporter for the U.S. House of Representatives follows the same practice.

In fact, Bob Levey mentioned that once when he quoted a fire chief as saying "I ain't never seen," Levey received 30 phone calls from outraged readers. Many firemen protested that if the chief had, in fact, said "ain't," Levey "should have 'mended' the quote so [the chief] didn't look bad."

By itself, tape recording can present transcribers with many puzzles, but this method is a useful backup to other methods for recording speeches, seminars, court proceedings, and the like. Today's professional court and convention reporters often turn on a tape recorder while they make shorthand, Stenotype, or Stenomask records. (A Stenomask reporter speaks into a masked microphone, repeating the proceedings, usually into a second tape recorder.)

Editing Transcripts

A thorough treatment of the matter of editing transcripts appears in a handbook (out of print), *English for the Shorthand Reporter*, put out by the National Shorthand Reporters Association (NSRA). The first two chapters explain why transcripts should be edited; the rest of the book tells how to do the work.

What happens to a transcript, of course, depends on what the client or employer prescribes; the result can range from a verbatim record to a heavily edited one.

When the reporter has a choice or when editing is specified, the NSRA book recommends that speeches be edited deftly and inconspicuously to correct "gross errors of English, inexact quotations from standard and accessible sources, endless sentences, false starts, immaterial asides, and other crudities," all done "so naturally as to escape the observation of the speaker himself."

In court reporting, the book strongly cautions against editorial changes that would in any way affect the testimony of witnesses or the substance of judges' charges and rulings.

Conclusion

Clearly, many people in the business of quoting believe that certain situations call for "tampering" with quotations ("editing quotations" is a kinder phrase). The motive may be consideration for the speaker or original writer and for the reader. Or the motive may be self-defense, to avoid being thought an illiterate, inaccurate, or insensitive reporter.

The NSRA book illustrates what can happen if editing isn't done. "Young man," said the statesman to the reporter who insisted that the record of the statesman's speech was accurate, "I don't *doubt* your accuracy; I *dread* it."

by Jim Taylor

Eight Steps to Good Copyediting

Good copyeditors know when to say, "Enough!"

Several years ago, a friend accosted me about an article of his that I had edited.

"That was a good article," he said. "But it wasn't *my* article anymore! There was hardly a sentence left in my own words." His comment still haunts me because it raises questions about the editor's role in shaping a manuscript. Of course, an editor must correct obvious errors, fix inconsistencies, and adhere to a style guide. I also believe an editor should make every word and phrase as good as can be. If I know that a better word can be substituted for the word the author wrote, should I not substitute it? But when and how does an editor cross the line between editing and rewriting? When should an editor say "Enough! No more!"?

Most editors recognize good writing almost instinctively and attempt—also instinctively—to bring everything they edit up to that standard. Recently, however, I have taught editing to some people who have no such instincts—business executives who need basic skills to edit their subordinates' reports and letters.

Teaching novices about editing has forced me to systematize the editing process. I've had to show people, step by step, how to do things that most editors do automatically. And that exercise, in turn, has taught me that there are various points at which an editor can say "Enough!"

As I edit, I find it helpful to remember that most editors also write. I then ask myself, as a writer, where would *I* balk at further editing? The following sequence of editing steps may help you, too, decide how much editing is enough.

Step 1. Shorten sentences. Nothing contributes so much to improved readability as inserting periods. Even without further editing, shorter sentences can cut a manuscript's Fog index in half. Yet the manuscript remains decisively the author's—often, not a single word needs to be altered.

Step 2. Cut verbiage. The act of shortening sentences frequently reveals fuzzy thinking—unnecessary qualifiers, redundancies, digressions, secondary ideas wedged into sentences. Cut them. Also cut all those foggy phrases (*in the event that, with reference to*, and *from the point of view of*) that can be replaced with simple short words (*if* or *for*) or eliminated.

After these editing steps, the major emphases remain in the author's own words. All editorial changes deal with peripheral words and phrases to which the author clearly gave minimal attention.

Step 3. Shorten words. Most long words consist of prefixes and suffixes grafted onto shorter words. Clear the pseudo-literary accretions from the root, and you'll have stronger prose. Suspect any word that ends in *-tion, -tive, -ality, -ousness*, or any combination thereof. Remember that editing doesn't have to preserve the same part of speech; the noun *implementation* can become the verb *implement*. These changes tighten the manuscript yet protect the author's vocabulary. With your skillful editing, many authors will not realize that their prose has been amended.

Step 4. Eliminate linking verbs. On a scale of 1 to 10, linking verbs have an energy level of 0. They create syllogisms: $a = b$, whether b is another noun, an adjective, or whatever. Syllogisms are static. They show no change, no growth, no action. Seek and destroy all uses of the verb *to be*. Use the verb's complement (part b of the $a = b$ equation) as an adjective. For example, change "The dog is red..." to "The red dog...." Or convert the *to be* construction into a verb requiring a direct object: "The vote is an affirmation..." becomes "The vote affirms...." Some syllogisms may be vital to logical argument or necessary for technical writing; most simply result from laziness.

At this halfway point in the eight-step editing process, the author will certainly perceive your influence but, without word-by-word study, may not yet recognize specific alterations.

Step 5. Convert negatives. Double negatives do not necessarily equal positives—for readers. Even single negatives can slow the reading process by requiring the reader to conceive of the positive before negating it: *nonvoting members* or *unreconstructed evidence.*

This step moves you, the editor, onto trickier ground. Changing a single negative into a positive may require substituting a different verb. Excising double negatives may subtly alter the meaning of the sentence. If you take the editing process this far, be aware that the author will recognize your changes and may become nervous and request explanations for your edits.

Step 6. Simplify vocabulary. Replace complex words with shorter, simpler synonyms. Change *annihilate* to *destroy*; change *vitreous* to *glassy.* In Step 3, you shortened words while retaining the author's roots—the noun *implementation* became the verb *implement.* In Step 6, you go farther, changing *implement* to *use.* Once again, precise connotations may shift subtly. Ask yourself if such shifts are worthwhile for improved readability.

In a sense, the editor becomes a translator from this step forward, replacing "puffed up" words and phrases with more comprehensible language. Although the intent and argument continue to belong to the author, the language becomes less recognizable as the author's own.

Step 7. Replace passive verbs. Verbs have different energy levels. Transitive verbs ("The dog bit the man") convey higher energy than intransitive verbs ("The dog bites") and passives ("The man was bitten by the dog" vs. "The man was bitten"). Only transitive verbs can be made passive. Change passives back into active verbs, and you've gone immediately to the highest energy level.

A word of warning: Some authors write in the passive voice from habit or ignorance. Politicians may prefer passives—if something is done, without anyone actually doing it, nobody can be held responsible. At this stage, the editor may subvert the author's intentions. Be careful.

Step 8. Restructure the manuscript. Any or all of the preceding steps may reveal weaknesses in the author's logic or organization that require major restructuring.

Restructuring is not necessarily the final step. Experienced editors may recognize flaws initially and restructure the manuscript immediately, tackling other amendments in the process. Manuscripts can sometimes be restructured without significantly altering the author's language. But novice editors should view structural editing as a last resort.

Because restructuring can drastically alter a manuscript's language, tone, and even thought patterns, the editor should discuss these changes with the author. Otherwise, the author may wonder, as my friend did, just whose manuscript this is.

This article was adapted with permission from the Freelance Editors Association of Canada's newsletter, Active Voice.

by Timothy Smith

On-line vs. On-paper Editing

On-line editing is here to stay— but you can't do it in the bathtub

Using paper and pencil to indicate proposed revisions will always have advantages over using cursor or mouse. The "equipment" required for the former is cheap and ubiquitous. The image of the marked page is easily copied or transmitted throughout the world, making review possible anywhere. The revision itself can then be done on any system—electronic, mechanical, manual, or even oral.

Paper is concrete. Hold a stack of it in your hand, and you can feel the size of the job. And it's easy to adapt paper to the task, the time, and the temperament. Paper permits a variety of notes or marks—from a gold seal to invisible ink to a private cipher to a drop of blood. You can tape paper to a wall, spread it out on the floor, write on it in the park, or ponder it in the bath. You can put several different versions of the same series of pages side by side. Try doing that on-line.

When pencil editing is done on printed text, it's plain where the text ends and the edit begins. One symbol can indicate many separate computer editing steps. But on-line editing that uses text characters to represent editing marks is far less distinguishable and therefore slower for an operator or text reviewer to interpret.

Computers that allow color images such as editing marks to be entered around text are available now, but a program that interprets the images as instructions and carries out the instructions is still beyond the range of the fanciest supercomputers.

Editing on a computer can feel like peering through one of those 25-cents-a-view telescopes found at scenic sites. If you want to look only where the telescope is aimed, and if you're the height the designer had in mind, the experience can be astonishing. But even the best, most "focused" text editing programs can't provide what a glance at a stack of paper can—a sense of the whole.

—Test Yourself—

What do the words *ancient, deficient, science, sufficient, counterfeit, either, neither, height, seize,* and *weird* have in common?

Answer on p. 96.

by Priscilla S. Taylor

EEI's Levels of Editing

Hints on how to distinguish one editing task from another

Editorial Experts, Inc. (EEI), a publications consulting firm in Alexandria, VA, divides editing into two broad categories—copyediting and substantive editing. For every job, a checklist is filled out specifying tasks needed in each category, and a second editor "reads behind" the first to maintain quality.

Substantive Editing

EEI substantive editing includes copyediting, rewriting, reorganizing, writing transitions, writing chapter or section summaries, eliminating wordiness, reviewing content for accuracy and logic, and ensuring the proper tone and approach for the intended audience. Substantive editing can also include helping plan and outline publications and consulting with authors and publishers.

Copyediting

EEI copyediting includes reviewing a "finished" manuscript (i.e., one that has undergone a substantive edit and client or author review of all substantive changes) for spelling, grammar, punctuation, consistency, and conformance to style. Copyediting includes checking the completeness, accuracy, and format of tables, bibliographies, and footnotes. It does not include rewriting or reorganizing.

The Checklist

To avoid confusion between clients and editors on just what is meant by a "light copyedit" or a "really substantive edit," EEI uses a checklist for each job.

Item by item, the checklist first details the minimum tasks for each job, including correction of spelling, grammar, and punctuation errors. A minimum edit also includes correction of inconsistencies, particularly in number style, capitalization, compound words, abbreviations, use of italics, lists, and alphabetical or numerical sequence.

The checklist specifies that editors rekey hard-to-read passages, make sure all pages are numbered in sequence, write a "cover memo" outlining what they did and did not do and listing their editorial style decisions and queries, and compile an alphabetical list of all words about which they have made a choice of treatment.

The checklist then itemizes additional copyediting tasks that a client may specify, including making a table of contents and a list of tables, making elements in a series parallel, clarifying pronoun antecedents, changing passive voice to active, eliminating the first person and sexist language, checking cross references, and explaining acronyms and abbreviations at first mention.

The final section of the checklist covers heavier, more substantive editing, rewriting, and related tasks, including reorganizing significant amounts of material; rewriting awkward, turgid, or confusing sections; reviewing a manuscript for portions that can be cut; and checking accuracy of content.

Editing Distinguished from Proofreading and Writing

EEI carefully separates editing from proofreading and writing.

Proofreading is defined as comparing a later stage of copy to an earlier stage, looking for typographical errors, poor type quality, and deviations from keyboarding or typesetting instructions. Proofreading includes queries on blatant errors and inconsistencies. "Editorial" proofreading includes extra attention to style matters and can include extensive queries.

To EEI, writing means starting almost from scratch, with no manuscript or with only notes, an outline, or a point of view from which to work. Writing can include research, interviews, publication planning, outline and draft preparation, summaries, and consultations.

by Elaine Sullivan

Editorial Proofreading vs. Copyediting

Understanding the differences and knowing when to do what

One manager asks that her proposal draft be proofread. What she means is, "Clean up the writing and make me look good in print." Another manager wants his technical report copyedited. You know him well enough to know that if you re-organize paragraphs or substitute simple words for technical noun strings, he'll be upset. The terms *copyediting* and *proofreading* are often confused by nonpublications people. Throw in the term *editorial proofreading*—a task that falls between copyediting and proofreading—and you really create confusion.

Editorial Experts, Inc., uses the following basic definitions to clarify these terms to our clients and to the editors and proof-readers who perform the functions. (Remember that jobs vary; therefore, your definitions of these terms may expand or contract to fit project and client requirements.)

The major differences among copyediting, proofreading, and editorial proofreading lie in *when* the tasks are done, *how* the work is marked, and *what* is marked.

A copyeditor works closely with an author or the substantive editor to prepare a manuscript for production. A copyeditor is con-cerned with the mechanics of the language—grammar and sen-tence structure—and is also sensitive to the style and flow of language. A copyeditor makes sure a manuscript conforms to predetermined style guidelines; looks for and corrects nonparallel construction, logic problems, and wordiness; eliminates smothered

87

verbs; and changes passive voice to active when appropriate. Copyeditors use editing marks and make the marks in text.

A proofreader reviews the manuscript *after* keyboarding and corrects the keyboarder's or typesetter's errors and any blatant grammatical problems that were missed in the copyediting step. Consequently, proofreaders work closely with keyboarders or typesetters. Proofreaders normally compare an original ("dead") manuscript against a corrected ("live") version. They use standard proofreading marks both in text to identify where the errors are and in the margins to indicate the needed corrections.

If a manuscript is rushed through its preproduction steps, a more thorough proofreading may be required after production. This step is called editorial proofreading and should not be confused with copyediting, which happens *before* production. Editorial proofreaders correct misspellings, grammatical errors, and style inconsistencies. They check cross references and numerical sequences, but they do not address logic problems or wordiness, nor do they reorganize or rewrite. They may point out problems with the flow of the language, but they do not make changes. Even though editorial proofreaders have the authority to make changes that regular proofreaders would only query, they do not have as much authority as copyeditors. Editorial proofreaders mark copy in the same manner as proofreaders—with proofreading marks in text and in the margins.

Ed. Note: Before readers dash off letters about our treatment of the terms *copyedit, copyeditor,* and *copyediting,* let us explain that Editorial Experts has chosen to flout convention and run these words together for consistency's sake.

by Mary J. Scroggins

That vs. Which: Is the Distinction Useful?

*Most knowledgeable writers
and editors say it is*

Language changes constantly, and change is usually good because it provides new opportunities for expression. However, change that results as the language evolves differs from change that results from oversight, ignorance, or expedience. The former enhances language; the latter restricts it and limits expression.

One example of language changing is the lessening distinction between *that* and *which* as gatekeepers of restrictive and nonrestrictive clauses, respectively.

Several months ago I spoke with a technical editor who insisted that a distinction is no longer being made in the use of *that* and *which* even by the most discriminating writers, editors, and readers. According to that editor, "Whichever you choose is fine, commas or no. Moreover, there is no reason for a distinction. Few people know the rule anyway."

I beg to differ. Although a change *has* begun to occur in the use of these words to introduce restrictive and nonrestrictive clauses, there has not yet been a large-scale abandonment of this perfectly valid and useful grammatical convention.

Let's review the traditional guidelines for the use of *that* and *which*.

Use *that* to introduce clauses that are restrictive (or essential), for example, clauses containing information that is *necessary* to understand the main idea of the sentence. Commas *do not*

89

precede or follow such clauses or other restrictive information. Example: "The sales meeting that was held in Peoria was not well attended."

Use *which* to introduce clauses that are nonrestrictive (or nonessential), for example, clauses containing information that is *not necessary* to understand the main idea of the sentence. Commas *do* surround these and other nonrestrictive clauses and information. Example: "The original 1989 budget, which reduced spending in many areas, has been modified by the new administration."

A memory device to help distinguish between *that* and *which* is "*that* defines, *which* describes."

These guidelines are easy to learn but not always easy to follow. Determining whether information is restrictive or nonrestrictive can be difficult. The editor should make the determination for the readers, who may not have sufficient expertise or information to do so. An editor who cannot determine whether the information in the clause is essential should query the author. Consider the following two sentences:

> *Nicotine that is addictive is a major ingredient in tobacco.*
> *Nicotine, which is addictive, is a major ingredient in tobacco.*

The first sentence indicates that some nicotine is nonaddictive and that only addictive nicotine is an ingredient in tobacco. The use of *that* and no commas alerts readers that all the information is essential and therefore necessary. The second sentence indicates that all nicotine is addictive. The use of *which* and commas alerts readers that the information surrounded by commas is nonessential (even if enlightening); it can be deleted with little or no effect on clear communication.

An easy way to decide whether information is restrictive or nonrestrictive is to determine whether the information in the clause applies to *all* people or things defined or described in the clause. If the information does apply to all, the clause is nonrestrictive (it does not set limits and adds no needed information) and requires commas. If the information *does not* apply to all, the clause is restrictive (it sets limits and adds needed information) and does not require commas. Using this technique, decide which of the following sentences is correctly worded and punctuated:

Rules of grammar, which are purposeless, should not be followed.
Rules of grammar that are purposeless should not be followed.

Are all rules of grammar purposeless? If you answer *yes*, the first sentence is correct and you are probably reading this article by mistake, because *which* (with commas) used to introduce the clause in this sentence indicates that *all* rules of grammar are purposeless. If you answer *no*, the second sentence is correct, because the restrictive clause introduced by *that* (no commas) signals the reader that *not all* rules of grammar—only the kind noted—are purposeless.

These two sentences convey markedly different messages. The first advocates total abandonment of rules of grammar; the second, judicious use of them. Obviously, the second sentence is correct and conveys the generally accepted view.

The choice of *that* or *which* with the attendant punctuation sets expectations for the reader. In making a choice, the editor distinguishes for the reader between necessary and unnecessary information.

Even if it is true that few people know the rule for using *that* and *which*, as the editor mentioned earlier contended, the suggested cure (to encourage or be guided by ignorance) is inappropriate. Some people do not know and therefore cannot follow the rules of subject-verb agreement, but "they is" is not about to come into vogue in formal, written communication. An appropriate remedy for a lack of knowledge is to educate readers through consistent usage.

English is not a throwaway language; it is an evolving, growing entity that is so rich in variations that the use of grammatical standards and conventions is essential for clear communication. The important consideration here is not tradition but standard usage, the reader's expectations resulting from long-established practice, and chiefly the usefulness of the form.

In some publications, it is already becoming acceptable to use *which* to introduce both types of clauses and to let the punctuation signal the distinction. In such cases, commas are omitted around restrictive clauses introduced by *which* and included around non-restrictive ones. The distinction is still being made, but made differently. This movement away from the traditional guidelines is an example of how language can evolve and still maintain useful and necessary distinctions. This form of linguistic evolution accommodates the need for distinctions and standards by developing new treatments before abandoning existing ones.

We can change the signals to readers only with caution and good cause—and neither expedience nor ignorance is good cause.

by Ann R. Molpus

The "Feel Bad" Rule

Most conscientious editors feel bad about "badly"

Most editors have a particular English teacher in their background who is remembered with fondness, respect—and fear.

One such teacher drummed into me the "feel bad rule." That is, the linking verb *to feel* requires a predicate adjective—*bad*, thus, "I feel bad," not "I feel badly." The latter use, my English teacher stressed, meant I had lost the feeling in my fingertips.

Yet I've noticed that word people whose command of the language I respect often say, for example, "I feel badly about missing your deadline." This usage also crops up in books by respected authors.

Why harp on this particular misuse? I harp because every time I hear someone say, "I feel badly," I think of Mrs. McDowell, my seventh grade English teacher, grimacing and rattling her charm bracelets in protest. *Webster's Dictionary of Usage and Style* notes with resignation that *bad* and *badly* are increasingly interchangeable, even in respectable circles. The usage experts polled in the *Harper Dictionary of Contemporary Usage* acknowledge the "feel bad rule," but the majority of them admit that when asked about their poor health, they avoid the issue and moan, "I feel lousy."

Thank goodness for traditionalists like Laurence Urdang, the editor of *Verbatim* newsletter and a former editor-in-chief of the *Random House Dictionary of the English Language*. In his book, *The Dictionary of Confusable Words* (New York, Facts on File Publications, 1988), Urdang calls this misuse a "contamination" and explains, "Those who wish to maintain a puristic style in language try to ensure the use of *bad* as an adjective and of *badly* as an adverb, modifying not only verbs but also adjectives and words (like participles) that act like adjectives: *a badly done painting.*" My English teacher would beam and say, "Quite right, Laurence, quite right."

Buy This Quality "Insurance"

Hints to keep quality high
and blood pressure low

Discussing editorial excellence at a *Folio* magazine Face-to-Face conference, several editors offered these suggestions for ensuring the quality of your editorial product:

▲ Have a clearly articulated vision of your publication and describe the vision in your editorial guidelines for contributors.

▲ Read and analyze the competition thoroughly and regularly.

▲ Know your readers and direct your editorial content to their concerns.

▲ Answer all letters to the editor to help readers feel part of the publication.

▲ Use reporters and freelancers who are good writers *and* experts in their field.

▲ Treat freelancers with respect.

▲ Pay attention to design.

Commandments for Copyeditors

The top ten do's and don'ts

1. Thou shalt not change the author's meaning.

2. Thou shalt not introduce new errors; especially shalt thou not change something correct to something incorrect.

3. Thou shalt change nothing except to improve it.

4. Thou shalt harken to thy instructions and do precisely what is expected of thee.

5. Thou shalt honor and obey those in charge over thee.

6. Thou shalt mark clearly and write legibly in a color that photocopies well.

7. Thou shalt protect the manuscript from rain, hail, wind, coffee, children, pets, and all things damaging.

8. Thou shalt meet thy deadlines.

9. Thou shalt assume nothing but shalt seek answers to all things doubtful or unspecified.

10. Thou shalt read and study the English language continually.

Test Yourself answers from page 8

1e, 2g, 3a, 4c, 5b, 6f, 7d, 8i, 9j, 10h

Test Yourself answers from page 38

1. lumen—electromagnetic radiation flux
2. maxwell—magnetic flux
3. gauss—magnetic induction (a maxwell/cm^2)
4. ohm—electrical resistance
5. roentgen—the quantity of x rays or gamma rays
6. volt—electromotive force
7. hertz—cycles of electrical frequency per second
8. farad—electrical capacitance
9. erg—work or energy
10. angstrom—a unit of length equal to one ten-billionth of a meter, usually used to measure light wavelengths
11. kelvin—temperature scale
12. stoke—viscosity

Test Yourself answer from page 84

All are violations of the old rule: "Place *i* before *e*, except after *c*, or when sounded like *a*, as in *neighbor* and *weigh*."

Contributors

Mara T. Adams is the former vice president of editorial services for Editorial Experts, Inc., Alexandria, VA. She is currently acting executive director for the Promotional Programs Group for PRACON, Reston, VA.

Molly Bentsen is the senior copyeditor at Human Kinetics Publishers, Champaign, IL.

Bruce O. Boston is a Washington, DC, writer and editorial consultant and the author of *Language On A Leash*, a collection of essays on language. Mr. Boston is a regular contributor to *The Editorial Eye* newsletter and a former editor of that publication.

Linda Jorgensen is the assistant editor of *The Editorial Eye* newsletter.

Marjorie Manwaring is an editor in the languages user education division of Microsoft Corp. in Redmond, WA.

Ann R. Molpus, a former magazine editor and corporate communications manager, is editor of *The Editorial Eye* newsletter.

Connie Moy is the proofreading division manager at Editorial Experts, Inc.

Morris A. Nunes is an attorney, counsel to Editorial Experts, Inc., and the author of five books and many articles on business and finance subjects.

Elizabeth L. Reed is a senior staff analyst at ARINC Research Corp. in Annapolis, MD, where she teaches technical writing to the professional staff, writes software user manuals, and produces marketing materials. She also teaches in George Washington University's Publication Specialist program.

Mary J. Scroggins is a freelance editor working in Washington, DC, and a publications seminar instructor for Editorial Experts, Inc. She was one of a team of editors who lent consistency to *The Iran-Contra Report.*

Peggy Smith is a writer and former *Editorial Eye* editor. She conducts proofreading seminars and contributes occasional articles to *The Editorial Eye*. She is the author of *Simplified Proofreading* and *Mark My Words: Instruction and Practice in Proofreading*.

Timothy Smith is a computer security and support officer at a major corporation in New York City.

Elaine Sullivan is vice president of administration for Editorial Experts, Inc.

Jim Taylor is the editor for Wood Lake Books in Canada. He teaches numerous workshops on writing and editing for the Freelance Editors Association of Canada (FEAC) and other groups. The workshop on eight-step editing is one of these.

Priscilla S. Taylor is a senior editor for Editorial Experts, Inc., and the editor of Phi Beta Kappa's quarterly *Key Reporter*. She is also a former editor of *The Editorial Eye* newsletter.

Index

Editorial Experts, Inc. (EEI), is a full-service publications consulting firm based in Alexandria, VA. EEI's services include writing, editing, proofreading, word and data processing, design and graphics, indexing, workshops for publications professionals, and temporary and permanent placement in the publications field. EEI plans and manages conferences and produces the publications arising from them. EEI also publishes the award-winning *Editorial Eye* newsletter and professional books for editors and writers.

For complete information on EEI's services, publications seminars, and books, please write to

Editorial Experts, Inc.
66 Canal Center Plaza, Suite 200
Alexandria, VA 22314-1538
703-683-0683
Fax: 703-683-4915

The Expert Editor was designed by Dana Mitchell of Editorial Experts, Inc., Alexandria, VA. It was set in Square Serif and Avant Garde using Ventura Publisher 3.0 and the LaserMaster 1000 to provide 1,000 dpi camera-ready copy. It was printed by Hagerstown Bookbinding & Printing Co. Inc., of Hagerstown, MD.

Do You Have What It Takes to Be an Expert Editor?

*T*he *Expert Editor* answers that question and more!! You'll find guidelines and suggestions to help you learn to

- ▲ Work effectively with freelancers and "volunteer" reporters
- ▲ Set productivity standards
- ▲ Establish an editorial policy
- ▲ Maintain editorial integrity
- ▲ Shape a useful, productive editorial board
- ▲ Edit "prima donna" authors
- ▲ Develop writers' guidelines

_____

The Expert Editor also includes dozens of hints and tips, including

- ▲ Eight steps to good copyediting
- ▲ Ten books every professional editor needs
- ▲ Eleven questions that ask, "Have I met the reader's needs?"
- ▲ Sixteen questions to clarify a writing assignment
- ▲ Twenty-seven questions to ask before you start any editorial project

...and much more!

51200

9 780935 012132

EDITORIAL EXPERTS, INC.

ISBN 0-935012-13-3